TEEN CUISINE
A BEGINNER'S GUIDE TO FRENCH COOKING

BY ABBY GAIL KIRSCH AND
SANDRA BANGILSDORF KLEIN
WITH ILLUSTRATIONS BY
peter max

ALL RECIPES TESTED BY
PARENTS' MAGAZINE FAMILY FOOD DEPARTMENT
PARENTS' MAGAZINE PRESS · NEW YORK

CONTENTS

I KITCHEN COUNT-DOWN 1
   Fundamentals of French Cooking

II THE GREAT CREPE CAPER 12
   Crêpes for All Courses

III EGG-O-MANIA 24
   Wild Ways with Eggs and Soufflés

IV THE MELTING POT 41
   High Dividend Stocks and Sauces

V HOW TO STAGE A LUNCH-IN 58
   Complete Light Meal Menus

VI FRENCH FEASTS 87
   Menus for Great French Dinners

VII COOK'S TOUR OF THE WORLD 125
   International Buffet Menus

VIII LET THEM EAT CAKE 149
   And Other Desserts

   KNOW YOUR UTENSILS 177
   A Cook's Catalogue of Equipment

   CONVENIENCE FOOD TABLE 179

   COMING TO TERMS 182
   A Cooking Dictionary

   INDEX 185

KITCHEN COUNT-DOWN

CHAPTER I

French cooking offers more satisfaction to the chef than you might suspect. It is a creative experience, a social asset, and a status symbol all at once, something like composing your own music, entertaining your friends with it at parties, and having Leonard Bernstein ask you for advice.

The French have been taking their food seriously, as a minor art form, for hundreds of years. They have mastered almost everything worth knowing about the mysteries of fine food. If your interest in food extends an inch beyond the menu at your local drive-in, you will enjoy discovering the secrets of cooking the French way.

This book lets you learn all about it, on any level you like. If you're a casual cook, you can at the very least learn to know your way around a French menu while picking up a few simple, sensational little specialties to concoct when the mood is on you. If (or when) your intentions are serious, you'll find a complete introduction

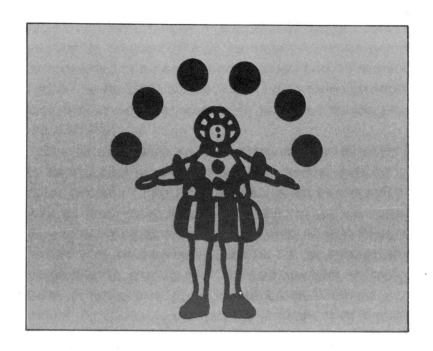

to basic French cooking techniques, as well as a thorough understanding of food that will make you a better cook all your life.

We've made everything as simple and complete as possible. Each recipe tells you where and how to substitute, cook-and-store in advance, and present the dish so it looks as good as it tastes.

You will learn authentic French cooking under modern American conditions. We understand perfectly that shallots are hard to get, truffles cost a fortune and you aren't likely to own a copper fish poacher. On the other hand, only in America can you count on strawberries in every season, a freezer in every refrigerator, and work-saving appliances in every kitchen. All the recipes deal with foods and equipment that are readily available, that save time, and that won't absolutely smash an ordinary budget.

A BRIEF HISTORY OF FRENCH CUISINE

A typical medieval European recipe probably began: "Take a crossbow and shoot anything that creeps, runs or flies." Meat obtained in this manner was often tough and gamey. Even domesticated livestock did not in any way compare with what we eat today. Corn-fed beef was unknown; for that matter, corn was unknown.

French cuisine originated with the discovery that juices from roasting meat could do something better than drip into the open fire. They could be used in cooking to improve the taste and texture. Thus began the long and fascinating history of French sauces. To this day, superb sauces are what set French cuisine apart from all others.

In the 14th century, a man named Guillaume Taillevente wrote the earliest French cookbook on record, "Le Viandier." In it he told how to stew a meat in its juices, creating the first ragout; and also how to thicken sauce with bread, the first thickening agent used.

In the 16th century, French cuisine took a giant leap forward when Catherine de Medici came from Italy to become the queen of Henry II. Catherine introduced a number of Florentine delicacies to the French court. Among them were grated Parmesan cheese, artichoke hearts, truffles, sweetbreads and tournedos or fillet steaks.

From then on, French chefs made their own history. In the 17th century, François Pierre de la Varennes originated the idea of reducing sauces and thickening them with a roux, or flour-butter mixture. In the 18th century, the great culinary luminary was Brillat-Savarin, who wrote a book of his accomplishments. In the 19th century, Antoine Carême advanced the cause of pastry, and Dumas Père contributed to the subject of salads.

You'll find lots of basic information in this chapter, and in the introductions to special sections such as soufflés, crêpes, sauces, and so on. If you are in doubt about the meaning of a cooking term or utensil, consult the Cooking Dictionary or the Cook's Catalog of Equipment. The Convenience Food Table can help you make time-saving substitutions, and there's information below that will answer your measuring questions. If you're not sure where to find something, the Index should tell you.

WHAT YOU SHOULD KNOW ABOUT CERTAIN FOODS

Eggs and egg whites: Eggs should be at room temperature when the whites and yolks are to be beaten separately for use in cakes or soufflés. Very stiffly beaten egg whites should stand in peaks, without sagging, and have a dry rather than a shiny surface. Never keep beaten egg whites. They should be beaten and folded in just before cooking. Egg yolks, well beaten, should be thick and lemon-colored.

Flour: There are two basic types of flour—all-purpose and cake flour—and they are *not* interchangeable. If the recipe does not specify which type of flour, it always means all-purpose. Most flour today comes pre-sifted and says so on the bag. If your flour is not pre-sifted, put it through a sifter or fine sieve before measuring. In measuring flour, spoon it lightly into the measuring cup; don't pack it down.

Butter and margarine: True French food is characterized by the taste of butter, but you may substitute margarine if you prefer it. Do not substitute whipped butter or margarine; its volume has been increased with air and it will not measure accurately unless the package gives

4

you equivalent amounts. When you measure butter by the cup, pack it down tightly in a dry measuring cup, level off with a knife and remove it with a knife or spatula. Salt butter is not recommended in frostings.

Confectioners' and brown sugars: Both should be sifted to remove lumps and to refine the texture. To measure brown sugar, pack it down tightly in a dry measuring cup. Powdered sugar, like most dry ingredients, should not be packed.

Prepared mustard: Where prepared mustard is called for, mustard imported from France gives the most authentic flavor. If it is not available, domestic mustard may be used instead.

Dried and fresh breadcrumbs: When a recipe calls for breadcrumbs, it means dried, unflavored breadcrumbs which can be bought prepared. Fresh or soft breadcrumbs can be made with any leftover bread by pulling out crumbs with fingers or fork, or by putting it in a blender.

Wines and Liqueurs: Although spirits are an integral part of authentic French cooking, there are times when food flavorings (such as rum, orange or brandy extracts) may be substituted if desired. Substitutions are indicated where feasible.

Melting chocolate: The three types of baking chocolate are unsweetened, semi-sweet and German sweet cooking chocolate. As chocolate burns easily, special care must be taken in melting it. Our favorite method is to place the chocolate in a custard cup, and let the cup stand in a small skillet of simmering water until the chocolate has melted.

Peeling and seeding tomatoes: To peel a tomato, first make a criss-cross cut on the skin at the bottom (not the stem) end. Then blanch by spearing a long fork through the stem end and plunging briefly into boiling water. This will loosen the skin and make it easy to peel away from the cuts you have made. Peaches can be peeled the same way. To seed the tomato, cut it in half and gently squeeze. The seeds will come out at once with the soft center, leaving the firm, meaty part ready for slicing. Save the centers to add to a sauce.

Tossing a salad: Salad greens should be rinsed and thoroughly dried with paper towels; or you can let them drain in a wire lettuce basket. They can be prepared in advance and stored, dry and tightly covered, in the refrigerator before adding dressing. When assembling the salad, first toss the greens with the dressing by lifting then turning lightly until all the greens are coated with dressing. Then add and toss the other ingredients.

Garlic: Fresh garlic comes in buds made up of three or more cloves. Don't mistake a whole garlic bud for a clove.

HOW NOT TO PLAN A MENU

Half the headache of giving a party, once you venture beyond the pretzels-and-soda school of entertaining, is coordinating an interesting, balanced and manageable menu. The luncheon, dinner, and international buffet chapters are all arranged in complete menus that satisfy these requirements. Still, there will be times when you want to do your own picking and choosing. Here are some things to avoid.

The super-duper drop-dead menu: This is a meal planned for an important occasion. It is a common mistake, at such moments of crisis, to offer dishes that are too plentiful, too elaborate and too fattening. The Roman orgy went out with the Sack of Rome; the groaning board results in groaning guests.

A truly sophisticated menu has a touch of understatement about it. The food is quietly excellent. The dishes do not crowd the plate or compete for attention. So beware of going overboard in your attempt to dazzle; there's a danger of drowning.

The lop-sided, too-much-of-a-good-thing meal: This occurs when the cook falls in love with one particular type of food, and the menu turns out to be variations on a theme. Every course comes out swimming in sauce; or flavored with fruit; or covered with something creamy. Even twice is too often to repeat an ingredient like onions, ham or mushrooms. In the same category are the all white, all brown or all wet meals.

The rules to follow: vary the flavor; vary the color; vary the texture. Texture includes creamy, crisp, crunchy, chopped, chewy and fluffy, so there's plenty to choose from.

7

As you climb the culinary ladder, remember to keep your sense of balance.

The unmanageable menu: This requires six hands, two heads and three ovens. It is characterized by a cook who is heard, clattering around in the kitchen, but rarely seen, except to serve and clear.

This problem can arise from two sources of bad menu-planning. One is having too many dishes requiring last-minute preparation. The other is having too many people for a menu requiring individual serving or scooping in the kitchen; for example, bowls of soup or balls of ice cream.

Antidotes: Don't schedule more than one dish requiring extensive last-minute preparation. And if you're having more than six people, plan dishes that can be served buffet-style or right from the table, rather than from the kitchen. Every menu in this book has a timetable, and every recipe has how-to-serve instructions. Consult both, even if you mix the menus around.

Moral: Cooking is like setting your hair; only the results should show.

SERVICE WITH A SMILE: DO'S AND DON'TS

The following rules apply especially when you're cooking for company, and are designed to let you and your guests relax and enjoy each other.

> *Do* have each course set up and ready to serve, dishes and all, before you start to eat.
> *Don't* dart in and out of the kitchen once everyone is seated.
> *Do* make use of trays for serving and clearing.
> *Don't* serve a lap-style dinner that is either runny or requires cutting with a knife.

8

Do ask a friend to help out with one or two non-grubby serving jobs, such as serving salad or beverage while you serve something else.

Don't let on that you've been slaving away for two days and nights and, are about to collapse from nervous exhaustion, even if it is true. Misery may love company, but company hates misery.

ADVANCE WORK

If you're planning a party, decide on your table setting and serving dishes at least a day before. Do as much day-ahead cooking as possible; each recipe tells you how much can be done in advance. Prepared food can be stored, covered, overnight in the refrigerator or up to two hours at room temperature. Prepare your garnishes the day before; they, too, can be refrigerated, in foil or plastic wrap. When cutting fruits like pears, bananas or apples in advance, sprinkle them with lemon juice to keep them from turning brown.

PRESENTATION

Foods, like people, are appreciated more when they look beautiful. This is the philosophy behind the art of presentation; and it is extremely important to French cooking. Each dish in this book is accompanied by its own suggestions for serving, but here are some general ideas to keep in mind.

Consider color in deciding upon a garnish, a serving dish, or an accompanying side dish; contrast is more effective than monotone. Choose a serving dish for size and shape in addition to color; leave the edge of the platter showing, but not so much that the food looks lost on it. Arrange food in an attractive pattern on the platter. Sliced meat should overlap neatly; raw vegetables can be arranged in a sunburst design, cooked vegetables or noodles may be mounded in the center or presented in a ring around another food, to mention just a few possibilities. Cookies and some finger foods look prettier when a paper doily is placed on the serving dish first.

The garnish itself can be thought of as an accessory, to be selected for shape and proportion as well as for color accent. It can be a sprinkling, as crumbled egg yolk or confectioners' sugar; a cluster, as watercress or a bunch of grapes; a sprig, as parsley; or a floweret as radishes or cauliflower. It can be an arrangement of geometric shapes such as tomato wedges, melon balls, green pepper rings, carrot sticks, pimiento arcs, pineapple cubes, toast triangles, and slices of orange, cucumber or olive. Almost any fruit, vegetable or nut can be used, in some form, to decorate some other food. So can some vivid sauces and jellies, like cranberry sauce or mint jelly.

Now that your imagination has been set loose, here's a word of caution: don't over-decorate. If you can't find the food for the garnish, you've gone too far. Remember what happened to the Gingerbread Man; he looked so much like a boy he forgot he was a cookie.

SEASONING TO TASTE

It is essential to get into the habit of tasting as you cook, and adjusting the seasoning as you think necessary. At the very least, this may mean adding more salt and pepper to the final dish. At a more creative level, it means adding more garlic, herbs, or other flavoring if you think it would improve the dish. You may even want to add an ingredient not called for. By all means, do so.

Personal preference varies greatly and is the foundation of creative cooking. The only caution is to be sure that herbs, onion or garlic are added early enough to get cooked rather than at the last moment. Only salt and pepper may be added at the end of the cooking period.

HINTS FOR EFFICIENCY IN THE KITCHEN

This is how to cut down on confusion, clutter and clean-up time. The following suggestions are part of good cooking technique, and will make the job go smoother.

Always read a recipe thoroughly before trying it, so you're sure you understand it.

Assemble all your ingredients before you begin, on a ready tray.

Pre-heat the oven at the time indicated in the recipe; usually the first step. It takes about 15 minutes for the oven to reach the right temperature.

Pre-measure ingredients before starting.

Have a sink full of sudsy water ready to soak each utensil as soon as it has been used. This saves scrubbing time later on.

Peel fruits and vegetables on a paper towel or wax paper. It's easier to dispose of the mess.

THE GREAT CREPE CAPER

CHAPTER II

Crêpes are delicate paper-thin French pancakes, as different from Grandma's griddle cakes as champagne is from ginger ale. They are usually rolled around a filling and covered with a sauce. Depending upon what you fill them with, crêpes are equally delicious for breakfast, appetizers, main courses or dessert.

Even apart from their versatility, crêpes are well worth learning to make. They look impressive, they taste heavenly (you don't have to *learn* to like them; unlike oysters, crêpes are love at first bite) and you can make them in advance. In fact, once you catch on to crêpes, you can keep them in the freezer ready to whip up into something spectacular whenever a sudden spectacle is needed.

Although crêpes may look hard to make, they're fun and easy to prepare with the following instructions.

Preparing the pan: A French crêpe pan is between 4" to 6" or 7" in diameter, made of heavy cast aluminum or iron, with shallow, flaring sides. You can buy a special pan, or you can use any small, smooth skillet with shallow sides.

Whichever type of pan you use, it should be prepared in the following way: Rub the pan with just enough oil to cover the bottom and sides and place it over medium heat. When the oil begins to smoke, turn off the heat and the pan is ready. Once you've treated it with the oil, don't wash it. You can wipe it clean with a paper towel when you've finished making the crêpes. If you do need the pan for other cooking chores, give it the oil treatment again before you make your next batch of crêpes.

What to watch out for: Crêpe batter should be thin, about the consistency of light cream. If the batter thickens, thin it with water, adding a few drops at a time until it's the right consistency.

If crêpes begin to stick to the pan, swirl a little butter around the edge of the pan as you cook.

Don't be discouraged if your first few crêpes aren't perfect. Usually this is because the pan isn't hot enough, the batter is too thick or you're using too much or too little batter at a time. You'll quickly develop the feel of making perfect crêpes. When you do, you may want to speed up the process by using two pans at a time.

Keeping them warm: If you're planning to use your crêpes immediately without baking them in the oven (for instance, as a dessert wrapped around preserves) you can keep them warm by stacking them on an oven-proof dish and keeping them in a 300° F. oven until you're ready to fill them.

Storing crêpes for later use: Line a flat-bottomed dish with wax paper. Place crêpes on wax paper, one at a time, using wax paper between each crêpe. Cover them well and keep them in the refrigerator up to two days, or in the freezer up to four months. Either way, let them warm to room temperature before filling them. If the recipe does not call for them to be browned in the oven, you can warm them in a skillet with a little butter.

It is also possible to freeze filled crêpes for two weeks *if the filling is cooked in advance.* Refrigeration is not usually recommended for pre-filled crêpes because they are likely to become soggy.

Assembling and baking crêpes: When you're ready to fill them, place the crêpes on a cookie sheet or work surface with the undersides (the spotty-looking sides) facing up. Spoon your filling into the center of each crêpe, and roll up loosely, away from you, jelly roll style. Most crêpes will then be transferred to a baking dish and either dotted with butter or covered with sauce, then baked in a 350° F. oven for 15 minutes, unless the recipe specifies otherwise.

BASIC CREPE RECIPE

(Makes about 12 to 18 6" crêpes)

3 eggs	2 cups milk
1½ cups all-purpose flour	2 tablespoons butter,
½ teaspoon salt	melted

Electric or hand-beating method: Break eggs into a mixing bowl and beat for 1 minute. Add flour, salt, milk and melted butter to the eggs and beat until smooth. If batter is lumpy, strain through a sieve.

Blender method: Place all ingredients in blender container and blend at top speed for 1 minute. Use rubber scraper to scrape batter from sides of container; blend 10 seconds longer.

Cover and refrigerate the batter for at least 2 hours. You can keep it up to 12 hours in the refrigerator, but it will thicken and need to be diluted with a little water.

After removing batter from the refrigerator, place the prepared pan over high heat. Melt ¼ teaspoon butter in the pan. When it begins to sizzle, the pan is ready for the batter.

Remove the pan from the heat and pour a scant ¼ cup batter into the middle of the pan. Quickly tilt the pan so that the bottom is thinly but evenly coated with batter. Pour any excess back into the bowl and return the pan to the heat.

The crêpe should be ready to turn as soon as bubbles form on the top and the underside is lightly browned, usually less than a minute. Flip the crêpe over with a pancake turner. The second side never looks as good as the first, so that's the side that gets the filling. Continue making crêpes in the same way until the batter is used up, adding butter to the pan after cooking every few crêpes.

LUNCH AND DINNER CREPES

When you serve crêpes as the main course at lunch, all the accompaniment they need are salad and rolls. For dinner, add a green vegetable, too. Two crêpes make an average serving. The same fillings may be used as hors d'oeuvres or as a late supper. All recipes make 6 main dish servings or 12 appetizers. The crêpes and filling can be prepared in advance, refrigerated separately and assembled at the last minute to bake.

CREPES POULET AUX CHAMPIGNONS
Chicken-Mushroom Crêpes
(Makes 6 servings)

12 crêpes
2 tablespoons cooking
    sherry (optional)
2½ cups Velouté sauce
    (p. 46)
1½ cups minced cooked
    chicken

½ cup chopped canned
    mushrooms, drained
2 teaspoons minced onion
1 teaspoon salt
½ teaspoon pepper
¼ cup grated Parmesan
    cheese

Add the sherry to the Velouté sauce and stir. Combine the chicken and mushrooms with ½ cup of the sauce plus the onion, salt and pepper.

Place 2 tablespoons of the mixture on each crêpe and roll up. Transfer filled crêpes to a shallow baking dish, cover with the remaining sauce, and sprinkle with grated Parmesan cheese.

Bake in a moderate oven (350° F.) for 20 minutes, then brown under the broiler for 5 minutes.

CREPES ASPERGES AU JAMBON

Crêpes with Asparagus and Ham

(Makes 6 servings)

12 crêpes

12 thin slices ham (preferably prosciutto)

12 canned asparagus
spears

2 cups Béchamel sauce
(p. 45)

Butter or margarine

¼ cup grated Parmesan
cheese

Top each crêpe with one slice of ham and one asparagus spear. Roll up. Transfer to a shallow baking
dish.

Cover the crêpes with Béchamel sauce, dot with
butter, and sprinkle with grated Parmesan cheese.
Bake in a moderate oven (350° F.) for 15 minutes,
then broil for 5 minutes more.

Note: Instead of asparagus, you can substitute 2 packages (10 oz. each) frozen spinach, cooked and drained.

CREPES AUX FRUITS DE MER   Crêpes with Crabmeat

(Makes 6 servings)

12 crêpes

2 cans (7 oz. each) crab-
meat

½ cup sliced fresh or
canned mushrooms

2 tablespoons butter or
margarine

1 teaspoon lemon juice

½ cup sour cream

¾ teaspoon salt

¼ teaspoon pepper

2 cups Mornay sauce
(p. 45)

¼ cup grated Parmesan
cheese

Drain crabmeat and remove cartilage, if any. If fresh mushrooms are used, wipe them clean before slicing, using both caps and stems. Sauté them in 2 tablespoons butter. When mushrooms are lightly browned, add the lemon juice. If using canned mushrooms, simply drain and add lemon juice; no cooking is required.

Combine the crabmeat, mushrooms and sour cream. Add salt and pepper.

Place 2 tablespoons of the mixture in each crêpe and roll up. Transfer to a shallow baking dish. Spoon the Mornay sauce over the crêpes and sprinkle with grated Parmesan. Bake in a moderate oven (350° F.) for 20 minutes; then brown under the broiler for 5 minutes.

Note: Cooked shrimp, lobster, halibut or tuna may be substituted for the crabmeat.

DESSERT CREPES

Dessert is the course that made crépes famous in the first place. Traditionally, they appear at the table in flames, to the music of violins. On page 20 we show you how to serve crêpes flambées. But first, here are three marvelous dessert crêpes minus the flames.

CREPES FRAMBOISE Raspberry Crêpes

(Makes 6 servings)

12 crêpes
2 jars (10 oz. each) raspberry jam

2 packages (10 oz. each)
   frozen raspberries,
   thawed and drained
¼ cup sifted confectioners' sugar

Heat the jam until warm. Fill each crêpe with 2 table-spoons of jam and roll. Keep filled crêpes warm in a 300° F. oven. Heat the thawed raspberries until they begin to simmer. Cover filled crêpes with raspberries, then sprinkle with confectioners' sugar. Serve warm.

CREPES PECHES A LA CREME
Peaches and Cream Crêpes

(Makes 6 servings)

12 crêpes
2 packages (10 oz. each)
   frozen sliced
   peaches, thawed

2 cups heavy cream,
   whipped
¼ cup sifted confectioners'
   sugar

Warm thawed peaches in a saucepan over medium heat. Spoon 2 tablespoons on each crêpe and roll. Keep filled crêpes warm in a 300° F. oven.

Sweeten whipped cream with sugar and serve with the warm crêpes.

CREPES FRAISES EN CREME GLACEE
Strawberry Sundae Crêpes

(Makes 6 servings)

12 crêpes
2 pints fresh strawberries
1 cup confectioners'
   sugar

1 tablespoon rum *or* 1 teaspoon rum extract
1 pint vanilla ice cream

Wash, hull and dry the strawberries; slice them in

half. Add confectioners' sugar and rum and let stand 1 hour.

Spoon 2 tablespoons of the fruit onto each crêpe and roll. Keep the filled crêpes warm in a 300° F. oven.

Stir the ice cream in a sauce boat until soft and serve it with the crêpes.

Note: Two packages (10 oz. each) of sliced frozen strawberries, thawed and drained, may be substituted for the fresh ones. They need not stand in sugar. Just add rum to the thawed strawberries and fill the crêpes as directed above.

DESSERT CREPES FLAMBEES

Here's where you finish a meal in a blaze of glory. For dramatic effect and for flavor, nothing surpasses food that is flamed.

The whole trick of flaming crêpes is to pour warmed liqueur over them and ignite it without singeing your eyelashes. The liqueur may be brandy or cognac, lemon extract or even a sugar cube soaked in brandy. Although the flames leap high, it is only the liqueur that burns, not the food. As the alcohol evaporates, the flame goes out, leaving a fabulous flavor on the crêpes.

Flaming is done quickly, at the last moment before serving, so have your crêpes ready and waiting at the table. Warm the liqueur over a low heat, using a burner-proof sauce boat if you have one. It looks more presentable than a saucepan when you take it to the table. At the table, pour the liqueur over the crêpes and ignite immediately, keeping your face away from the flame.

A few don'ts: Don't warm the liqueur over high heat or the alcohol will burn away before you can ignite it.

Don't carry a flaming dish to the table.

Don't deprive the others of seeing the fireworks. If you must flame the crêpes at the stove, have everyone come and watch.

Don't blow out the flames; they only last a few seconds.

CREPES JUBILEE
(Makes 6 servings)

12 crêpes, kept warm in the oven
2 tablespoons cornstarch
1 cup sugar
2 cups water
2 cans (1 lb. each) dark sweet pitted cherries
1 pint vanilla ice cream
¼ cup cherry liqueur *or* brandy

Combine the cornstarch, sugar and water in a saucepan, stirring constantly over medium heat until the mixture is clear. Drain the cherries and add them to the mixture in the saucepan. Stir gently with a wooden spoon until the mixture thickens to the consistency of heavy syrup.

Fill each crêpe with 2 tablespoons of ice cream and roll. Transfer the filled crêpes to a heated serving dish and top with the warm cherry mixture. Warm the liqueur (or use 2 tablespoons rum extract) in a burner-proof sauce boat and pour over the crêpes. Ignite immediately and serve.

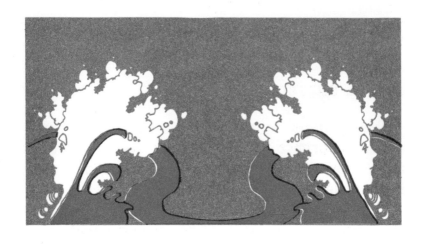

CREPES CHOCOLAT ET ORANGE
Crêpes with Chocolate-Orange Sauce
(Makes 6 servings)

12 crêpes
1 cup Chantilly cream (p. 175)
3 tablespoons chopped pistachio nuts (optional)
1½ cups prepared fudge sauce

2 tablespoons sugar
2 tablespoons butter or margarine
¼ cup orange juice
3 tablespoons orange liqueur *or* 1 teaspoon orange extract

Fold the pistachio nuts into the Chantilly cream.

Fill each crêpe with 2 heaping tablespoons of the Chantilly cream mixture and refrigerate until serving time.

Just before serving, start heating the fudge sauce. In a separate burner-proof sauce boat, combine the sugar, butter and orange juice. Stir constantly over moderate heat until the sauce turns a rich golden brown. Add the liqueur, warm another 3 seconds and ignite.

When the flame dies, stir in the hot fudge sauce and spoon over the filled, chilled crêpes.

CREPES SUZETTE

(Makes 6 servings)

This is one of the most famous dishes in the world. The taste cannot be described or even imagined; it must be experienced. Ideally, the crêpes are assembled at the table in a chafing dish.

12 crêpes
½ cup butter
1 cup confectioners' sugar
1 cup orange juice

2 teaspoons grated orange peel
¼ cup brandy or cognac
3 tablespoons orange liqueur *or* 1 teaspoon orange extract

Fold each crêpe in half, and then in half again, so they look like little wedges. Keep them warm in a 250° F. oven.

Cream the butter and confectioners' sugar until light and fluffy. Add the orange juice and orange peel and mix well.

Just before serving, transfer the butter-orange mixture to a chafing dish or skillet and place over moderate heat until bubbly. Add the folded crêpes. When the crêpes are warm, add the brandy and liqueur, and continue heating another 30 seconds. Ignite. Serve at once, spooning the sauce over each portion of crêpes.

EGG-O-MANIA

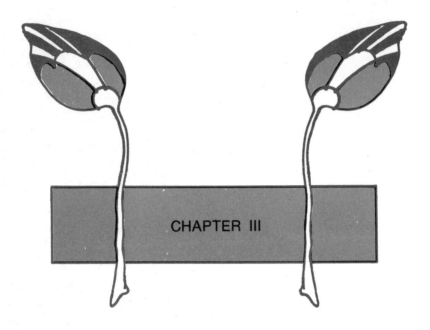

CHAPTER III

The interesting thing about eggs, apart from their usefulness in producing chickens, is their versatility. What other food can be eaten for breakfast, supper or dessert; can be served hot or cold, hard or soft, stuffed or puffed up into a glorious soufflé; is always on hand in the refrigerator, and is good for you besides?

In this chapter you will learn the art of the omelette and the secret of soufflés. You'll also learn the right way to make everyday eggs of the poached-boiled-scrambled school. (Yes, there *is* a better way to boil an egg!) These not only taste better when made properly, but are the starting points for some very good variations.

OEUFS POCHE Poached Eggs
(Makes 4 servings)

If you have an egg poacher, use it. If not, this method should work as well. The eggs may be served on toast, or they may be transformed into something as special as Eggs Benedict. The French use a lot of water, but we like this method better.

Put enough water into an 8-inch skillet so that it is 2″ to 3″ deep. Add ½ teaspoon *vinegar,* if desired. Heat the water to just *below* the boiling point. One at a time, break each egg into a custard cup and slide the egg from the cup into the water. When all the eggs are in the pan, let the water come to a simmer; then cover the pan and remove from the heat. Let the eggs sit in the water until the whites are firm, about 3 to 5 minutes. Remove them with a slotted spoon.

If the eggs are not to be served immediately, place them in cold water to stop the cooking. When you're ready to use them, trim the ragged edges of white and place the eggs in hot water for a minute to warm them.

VARIATION ON A POACHED EGG

OEUFS BENEDICTINE Eggs Benedict
(Makes 6 servings)

Butter	6 slices boiled ham
3 English muffins, split and lightly toasted, (or 6 slices lightly toasted white bread, cut in rounds)	6 poached eggs
	1½ cups warm Hollandaise sauce (p. 53)

Butter the muffins. Place on a cookie sheet, buttered sides up, and cover each round with one slice of ham and one warm poached egg. If you have individual ramekins, transfer one round to each ramekin, otherwise keep them on the cookie sheet.

Cover each egg generously with the warmed Hollandaise sauce and broil 6″ to 8″ from heat for 3 to 5 minutes, or until top is bubbly. Serve at once.

OEUFS BROUILLE   Scrambled Eggs
(Makes 2 servings)

Scrambled eggs are widely misunderstood because they usually appear either spongy or lumpy, hence horrible. When they are properly cooked, they are soft and creamy and really delicious. The secrets of perfect scrambled eggs are adding water, cooking slowly, and stirring constantly. Also, don't make too many eggs at once; six in a large pan are the maximum, but four in a medium pan are better. If you object to the little white spots in scrambled eggs, remove them with a fork before mixing.

4 eggs	1 teaspoon salt
1 tablespoon cold water	¼ teaspoon pepper
	1 tablespoon butter

Break eggs into a mixing bowl, add water, salt and pepper, and mix well with a fork or wire whisk.

Melt the butter in a medium (8″) skillet over moderately low heat. When the butter is sizzling (but just before it browns), pour the eggs into the skillet. If the butter is hot enough, they should begin setting at once; if they set too rapidly, lower the heat. Stir *constantly;* do not let the parts that have set stay on the bottom of the skillet. As soon as the eggs are set, but still moist, *remove them from the skillet,* otherwise the hot skillet will continue to cook them even when it is removed from the heat. Serve immediately.

VARIATIONS ON SCRAMBLED EGGS

You can add almost anything you like to scrambled eggs, or you can garnish them with sausages, bacon, asparagus or broiled tomatoes. The following suggestions are added to the basic recipe before cooking; but the cheese is added just before removing from the heat.

Herbs: ¼ teaspoon *each* dried parsley and chives, or 1 teaspoon each fresh. (Other herbs can be added or substituted if you like.)

Mushrooms: ¼ cup chopped canned mushrooms, well drained

Ham: ¼ cup diced cooked ham

Cheese: 1 tablespoon grated Swiss cheese, added just before removing the eggs from the heat.

OEUFS DUR Hard Cooked Eggs
(Makes 6 servings)

Everyone knows how to boil an egg, but here is a method that avoids cracked shells and a rubbery texture. The cooked eggs can be refrigerated for 3 days, either in their shells or in a plastic bag.

6 eggs   Water to cover

Place eggs in a medium saucepan with enough water to cover them. Bring the water to a rapid boil and cover. Remove from the heat and let stand 20 minutes. Plunge the eggs into cold water and peel, if they are to be used at once.

THE ART OF THE OMELETTE

A French omelette takes some practice to perfect, but it is worth the effort. It is always tender and light with a moist center. It is never dry. An omelette can be served plain, or filled with a variety of foods. After you have absorbed the technique, the actual preparation time is only a few minutes.

DO'S AND DON'TS FOR A SUCCESSFUL OMELETTE

Do have the eggs at room temperature before you begin.

Do prepare the pan as described on p. 29.

Do be sure the butter or margarine is hot enough before adding the eggs.

Do have a plate ready and waiting to receive the omelette.

Don't use less than 2 or more than 4 eggs.

Don't cook the eggs too long.

Don't keep the eggs in the pan after they're cooked, not even a minute.

PREPARING THE PAN

Use an omelette pan if you have one, or any heavy, medium-size skillet (7" to 8"). Scrub it with steel wool, rinse and dry well. Pour enough salad oil into the pan to coat the entire surface. Heat the oil over a high flame until it is almost smoking. If possible, let it remain in the pan overnight. Wipe (don't wash) the oil off with a paper towel before using. The purpose of all this is to make sure the omelette will slide out of the pan in one piece.

OMELETTE AU NATUREL   Basic Omelette
(Makes 2 servings)

4 eggs at room temperature	¼ tablespoon salt
	Dash of pepper
1 tablespoon cold water	1 tablespoon butter

Mix the eggs, water, salt and pepper thoroughly with a fork or wire whisk. Melt butter in the pan over high heat until sizzling *but not brown*.

The first drops of egg should hiss as they are poured into the pan; if they don't, wait a few seconds before adding the rest.

As the eggs begin to set, scrape the set portions from the edge of the pan toward the center, using the tip of a fork. At the same time, tilt the pan so the uncooked egg can seep down to the bottom.

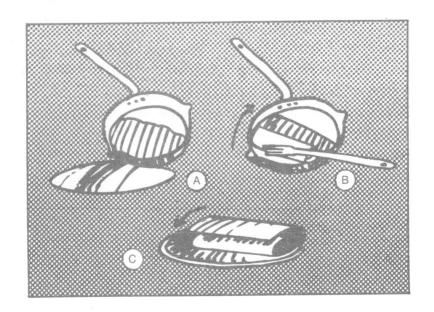

With the fork in one hand and the pan handle in the other, keep scraping and tilting for several seconds, always over high heat, until the bottom is set and the top is soft and moist.

Tilt the pan toward the waiting plate so the omelette begins to slide down (Illustration A). With the fork, fold the downward edge of the omelette toward the center of the pan (Illustration B).

Now, rest the edge of the pan on the plate and turn the pan upside down so the omelette forms a second fold as it slides onto the plate (Illustration C).

If everything has gone well to this point, the omelette will be loosely folded into thirds, with two edges overlapping in the middle.

Serve immediately, cutting it in half at the table for 2 portions. Garnish with sprigs of parsley.

VARIATIONS ON AN OMELETTE

All the following suggestions except the herbs are for

fillings, which are placed on the omelette just before it is folded. Fillings should be at room temperature, or they can be warmed briefly just before making the omelette. Each filling is for a 4-egg omelette.

Asparagus: Add 3 canned asparagus spears.

Cheese: Add 3 tablespoons grated Swiss cheese.

Ham: Add 3 tablespoons diced cooked ham.

Herbs: Add 1 teaspoon fresh or frozen chives or tarnagon (or ¼ teaspoon dried) to the uncooked eggs.

Mushroom: Add 3 tablespoons canned, drained, chopped mushrooms.

Seafood: Add 3 tablespoons chopped cooked shrimp or crabmeat.

COMBINED VARIATIONS ON AN OMELETTE

There is no limit to the combination of foods and flavorings you can concoct for filling an omelette. It depends only on what you like, and what you can find around the house—leftovers are a good place to start. The only rules are to *cook* the fillings and to *flavor* them. For flavorings, consider sautéed onion, garlic or curry powder and herbs, as well as salt and pepper. Foods like ham, bacon or caviar are like seasonings by themselves. The following combinations are just to give you the idea; however, the *main* idea is to be inventive. Remember 3 tablespoons will fill a 4-egg omelette; and have the filling warm and waiting before you make the omelette.

Chopped Spinach with Bacon and Cheese

Chicken Livers, Onion and Garlic

Crab with Curry and Sour Cream (Don't boil the cream!)

Eggplant, Tomato and Basil

And for a deluxe topping for a plain omelette, served cold, add red caviar and sour cream.

SOUFFLES

A soufflé, if you haven't had the pleasure of eating one, is a light main dish or dessert that puffs up into a great, airy mound. It is served hot from the oven; delicately crisp and golden brown on top, tender and fluffy inside.

You do not have to be an accomplished French chef to create a soufflé. Since few people know this, you can easily carve a reputation as a cook on the basis of a few successful soufflés. They are simple to make, once you understand the ground rules.

UNDERSTANDING SOUFFLES

A soufflé is a mixture of white sauce, flavoring or purée, and egg yolks (collectively known as "the base") into which stiffly beaten egg whites are folded. When baked, it puffs to about three times its original volume. This happens because the air beaten into the egg whites expands in the heat of the oven. It also collapses again when it cools, which leads to the well-known rule: "The guests wait for the soufflé; the soufflé does not wait for the guests." Obviously, properly prepared egg whites are critical to the success of the soufflé.

HOW TO PREPARE EGG WHITES FOR A SOUFFLE

1. Have your eggs (preferably large ones) at room temperature before you begin.
2. Separate the eggs very carefully; don't let any yolk slip into the whites or they won't puff properly.
3. Be sure your mixing bowl is free of grease.
4. Add a pinch of cream of tartar or salt to insure stiff whites; add it when the whites are beaten to a foam (about 30 seconds).

5. French chefs beat their whites with a jumbo whisk, but they have strong arms. Unless you do, too, we suggest using an electric mixer or rotary beater. Make certain the whites on the sides of the bowl get beaten too. Beat at a moderate speed until foamy, then finish at high speed until stiff.

6. The whites are stiff when the peaks can stand by themselves without sagging.

7. Add 2 tablespoons of the beaten white to the soufflé base and stir well before folding in the rest of the whites. This is important because it lightens the base and makes folding easier.

8. Fold the whites into the base, *never stir or beat.* Don't overfold; the mixture should look streaky rather than uniformly smooth. (Check the Glossary, p. 183, for exact instructions on Folding.)

9. Do not let the soufflé stand after the whites have been folded in; it must be baked immediately.

GENERAL HINTS FOR MAKING A SOUFFLE

1. The soufflé base may be made in advance. If refrigerated, bring it to room temperature before adding the whites.

2. Before adding egg yolks to a hot base, warm the yolks by stirring a little of the base into them; otherwise the yolks will scramble.

3. Use a 6-cup (1½-quart) soufflé dish for these recipes, which serve four; or use an equivalent deep, straight-sided, oven-proof dish.

4. Prepare the soufflé dish by greasing the sides and bottom well with butter, then sprinkling with grated cheese for a luncheon soufflé or granulated sugar for a dessert soufflé. This can be done in advance.

5. Bake the soufflé on the middle rack of a pre-heated oven.

6. Once the soufflé is in the oven, walk softly, no running, jumping or door-slamming. Don't even open the oven to peek for at least 20 minutes or a draft may stop the soufflé from rising.

MAIN DISH SOUFFLES

Soufflé as the main course for lunch or supper is usually made with cheese and/or a vegetable or seafood. You can whip up the whole thing on the spot, or you can do everything but the egg whites earlier in the day. The whites must always be beaten and folded in just before the soufflé goes in the oven. Add rolls and salad and you're all set.

SOUFFLE AU FROMAGE   Cheese Soufflé
(Makes 4 servings)

¼ cup butter	1 cup (¼ lb.) grated Swiss
¼ cup flour	or Cheddar cheese
1 cup scalded milk	4 egg yolks
½ teaspoon salt	5 egg whites
⅛ teaspoon white pepper	⅛ teaspoon cream of tartar
½ teaspoon dry mustard	or salt
(optional)	

Preheat the oven to 375° F. Grease the 1½-quart soufflé dish with butter and sprinkle with 1 tablespoon of the grated cheese.

Melt the butter in a small saucepan. Remove from the heat and blend in the flour. Return to a moderate heat and cook, stirring, 2 to 3 minutes, being careful not to brown the flour.

Still stirring briskly with a wooden spoon or a whisk, add the boiling milk. The mixture will thicken immediately.

Add the salt, pepper and mustard and cook 1 minute; it will now be very thick. Add the grated cheese and stir until melted and blended. Add the egg yolks, which have been warmed as directed above in the General Hints.

About 45 minutes before serving, beat egg whites until foamy. Add the cream of tartar or salt, and beat until the whites stand in stiff peaks. Blend 2 tablespoons of the white into the base and stir well. Gently fold the rest of the white into the mixture. Pour into the prepared dish and bake 35 minutes, until puffed and browned. Serve immediately.

SOUFFLE D'EPINARD Spinach Soufflé
(Makes 4 servings)

A vegetable soufflé can be a side dish with a simple meat course, as well as a main dish by itself. As a side dish, it will make 4 to 6 servings.

Soufflé base:

¼ cup butter
¼ cup flour
1 cup scalded milk
½ teaspoon salt
⅛ teaspoon nutmeg

1 cup grated Cheddar
   cheese
4 egg yolks
5 egg whites
   Dash of cream of tartar or
   salt

Spinach mixture:

1 tablespoon butter
1 tablespoon minced shal-
   lot or white onion

1 package (10 oz.) frozen
   chopped spinach,
   cooked and well-
   drained

¼ teaspoon salt

Preheat oven to 375° F. Butter the 1½-quart soufflé dish and sprinkle with 1 tablespoon of the cheese.

Soufflé base: Melt the butter in a small saucepan. Remove from heat and stir in flour. Stir in boiling milk, add salt and nutmeg and blend.

Return to moderate heat for 1 minute, stirring until thick. Add the grated cheese, stirring constantly until melted.

Add the warmed egg yolks as directed in General Hints (p. 33), and set aside.

Spinach mixture: Melt the butter in a small saucepan. Cook the shallots in the butter for 2 minutes over moderate heat.

Add the cooked spinach and salt and cook, stirring, 2 to 3 minutes until all the butter has melted. Add the mixture to the cheese base and blend.

About 45 minutes before serving, beat egg whites until foamy. Add the cream of tartar or salt, and beat until stiff. Fold into the base as directed in General Hints, pour into the soufflé dish, and bake 35 minutes until puffed and browned. Serve immediately.

VARIATIONS ON A MAIN DISH SOUFFLE

Follow the recipe for a Cheese Soufflé, substituting any of the following for the cheese, or combining any of them with ¾ cup of grated cheese:

Fish or seafood: 1 cup drained flaked tuna, salmon or crabmeat; cooked chopped shrimp or lobster.

Vegetables: 1 cup finely chopped (cooked or canned) mushrooms, asparagus or broccoli.

DESSERT SOUFFLES

A dessert soufflé is a fitting finish for the most elaborate dinner. It can also turn a tuna salad supper into a banquet. It ranks among the great, super-gourmet desserts of the world.

Since a dessert soufflé bakes for 35 minutes, it must go into the oven just before you sit down to the main course. To avoid last-minute frenzy, it is wise to prepare the base earlier in the day and keep it covered. A few minutes before dinner, you can beat the egg whites, fold them into the base, and pop it into the oven. By the time the main course is eaten and cleared, the soufflé should be ready to serve. If you're planning to serve a dessert sauce with it, by all means have that ready in advance, too.

SOUFFLE A LA VANILLE   Vanilla soufflé
(Makes 4 servings)

When you get tired of this, which may be never, a simple switch can turn it into a lemon, orange or coffee soufflé. All four flavors can be varied by serving different dessert sauces with them (see the Dessert Chapter, for sauces).

¾ cup milk	2 tablespoons butter
3 tablespoons flour	2½ teaspoons vanilla
⅓ cup sugar	5 large egg whites
4 large egg yolks	Dash of cream of tartar or salt

Preheat the oven to 375° F. Grease the 1½-quart soufflé dish with butter and dust with sugar.

In a small saucepan, off the heat, stir ¼ cup of the milk into the flour until smooth. Vigorously beat in the rest of the milk and the sugar. Cook over moderate heat, stirring constantly with a whisk or wooden spoon, until the mixture comes to a boil and thickens.

Remove from heat. Stir for 2 minutes to cool slightly, and beat in the warmed egg yolks as directed in General Hints (p. 33). When well blended, beat in the butter and vanilla.

Beat the egg whites until foamy, add the cream of tartar or salt, and continue beating until stiff. Blend 2 tablespoons of the egg white with the base, then fold in the remainder of whites.

Pour into the soufflé dish and bake on the middle rack of the oven for 35 minutes, until puffed and golden brown. Serve immediately, plain or with dessert sauce.

VARIATIONS ON A VANILLA SOUFFLE

Substitute any of the following for the vanilla:

38

Lemon Soufflé: 3 tablespoons lemon juice plus ½ teaspoon vanilla.
Orange Soufflé: 3 tablespoons orange liqueur or 1 teaspoon orange extract plus ½ teaspoon vanilla
Coffee Soufflé: 2 tablespoons powdered instant coffee
plus ½ teaspoon vanilla

SOUFFLE AU CHOCOLAT Chocolate Soufflé
(Makes 4 to 6 servings)

Even if you had two heads, both of them ugly, you
could become a social success overnight by serving
this to your friends; that's how delicious it is. It is also
somewhat trickier to get right than other soufflés, because chocolate is heavy and a soufflé must be light.
We have solved the problem by using cornstarch instead
of flour in the base and by adding an extra egg white.
Still, go over your preliminary instructions very carefully;
every little trick helps in getting the soufflé to rise. If it
doesn't, you'll be left with a very rich, hot, pudding-like
dish. That isn't so terrible, but it isn't exactly a soufflé,
either.

2 squares unsweetened chocolate	5 egg whites
1 tablespoon cornstarch	Dash cream of tartar or salt
5 tablespoons sugar	1 tablespoon sugar
⅔ cup milk	1 tablespoon sifted con-
2 teaspoons vanilla	fectioners' sugar
3 egg yolks	

Preheat the oven to 400° F. Butter the 1½-quart
soufflé dish and dust it with sugar.
Place the chocolate in a custard cup, and put the
cup into a small skillet of simmering water until the

chocolate has melted completely, about 5 to 7 minutes.

In a small saucepan, off the heat, blend the corn-starch, sugar and milk until smooth. Cook over moderate heat, stirring constantly with a whisk or wooden spoon, until the mixture boils and thickens.

Remove from the heat and beat in the vanilla and melted chocolate. Add the warmed egg yolks carefully, as directed in General Hints (p. 33) and set aside.

Beat the egg whites with the cream of tartar or salt until peaks begin to form. Add the tablespoon of granu-lated sugar and beat until stiff. Stir 2 tablespoons of the egg white into the base. Fold the remaining egg whites into the chocolate base and pour into the soufflé dish. Place on the middle rack of the oven and turn the heat down to 375° F. Bake 35 minutes. Sprinkle the top with confectioners' sugar and serve plain, with whipped cream or with another dessert sauce.

You may alter the flavor by adding 2 teaspoons of powdered instant coffee or coffee liqueur, orange liqueur or rum to the chocolate base.

THE MELTING POT

CHAPTER IV

Stock or Fonds de cuisine is literally the foundation of French cookery. It is made by simmering meat, bones and vegetables in a large kettle of water for many hours until the liquid becomes rich and concentrated. Its use, instead of water, in appropriate sauces, soups and other dishes often spells the difference between the merely good and the truly great.

Because it is used as a base in preparing food, the stock itself will taste bland. Strongly flavored seasonings such as dill and tarragon are to be avoided; even salt should be used sparingly. You'll have time to get creative with herbs and spices when you prepare the final dish.

The two basic stocks you will need are a brown stock with a meat base for use in brown sauces, and a white stock with a chicken base for use in white sauces.

One batch of stock will be enough for many dishes. You can store it conveniently in the freezer in the form of frozen cubes, or in tightly wrapped plastic bags. Four cubes melt down to ½ cup of liquid. If you use plastic bags, measure one or two cups of chilled stock to a bag. If you should defrost more than you need, bring the stock to a boil before re-freezing it.

Stock can also be stored in the refrigerator for a short time, if you boil it once a week.

FONDS BRUN   Brown Stock
(Makes 2 quarts)

2 pounds beef soup meat

2 pounds beef marrow bones

1 pound veal bones

½ cup carrots cut in large pieces

½ cup onion cut in large pieces

½ cup celery, cut in large pieces

Cold water

3 to 6 sprigs parsley

1 bay leaf

1 tablespoon salt

Preheat oven to 450° F. Cut the meat into 1" pieces and place it in a roasting pan along with the bones and diced vegetables. Roast, uncovered, for 45 minutes or until the bones, meat and vegetables have browned, turning 2 or 3 times during the cooking.

Fill a 6-quart kettle with 4 quarts of cold water. Add the roasted beef, bones and vegetables, using a slotted spoon to remove them from the pan.

Drain off and discard all the fat from the roasting pan, then add 1 cup of cold water to the pan; cook over moderate heat for one minute, scraping up all the browned bits.

Add the scrapings and water to the stock pot, along with the parsley, bay leaf and salt. Partially cover the stock pot; bring to a boil. Reduce heat; simmer 2 hours.

Strain the stock through a fine sieve and cool to room temperature. Refrigerate until the fat has congealed on the surface. Remove the fat, and store the stock in freezer or refrigerator for later use.

FONDS BLANC DE VOLAILLE   White Chicken Stock
(Makes 2½ quarts)

4 quarts cold water
1 stewing chicken (about
    4 lbs.) quartered
1 pound chicken giblets
½ cup carrots cut into
   large pieces

½ cup onions, cut into
   large pieces
½ cup celery, cut into
   large pieces
3 sprigs parsley
1 bay leaf

2 teaspoons salt

Put all ingredients into a 6-quart kettle and bring to a boil. Skim off the thick foam that will form on the surface. Reduce heat and simmer, partially covered, for 2½ hours.

Remove the chicken; you can use it to make chicken salad, or maybe Chicken-Mushroom Crêpes (p. 16). Strain the stock through a fine sieve and cool to room temperature. Refrigerate several hours and remove all the fat which has congealed on the surface. Store stock for later use in freezer or refrigerator.

QUICK BROWN OR WHITE STOCK
(Makes 1½ cups)

3 cups beef or chicken
   bouillon
½ cup onions, finely diced
½ cup carrots, finely
   diced

½ cup celery, finely
   diced
3 sprigs parsley
¼ bay leaf

You may use canned bouillon or reconstituted bouillon cubes in this sauce. Place all ingredients in a medium saucepan and bring to a boil. Reduce heat and simmer 30 minutes. Strain through a fine sieve.

EMERGENCY BROWN OR WHITE STOCK

Just use canned or dehydrated bouillon. Don't feel guilty about it; it's still better than using plain water. Dehydrated bouillon comes in powder or cubes and is diluted according to the directions on the package. It's handy to have around anyway. For instance, pop a cube into the pot when you cook rice, or do the same thing to revive a watery soup. There is no watery soup in this book, but it can happen to anyone who hates to throw out unused chicken giblets and necks.

GETTING DOWN TO SAUCES

A master French chef has over 200 sauces at his command, most of them variations on a few basic themes. The complete range includes simple melted butter sauces, oil-and-vinegar sauces, and egg-based sauces (such as Hollandaise and Mayonnaise); but by far the largest category are the brown and white sauces made with a roux base.

Roux—the Base of Brown and White Sauces: A roux consists of a fat, usually butter or oil, blended with a thickening agent such as flour or cornstarch. The flour or cornstarch, besides thickening the sauce, also gives it a smooth, glossy texture. The roux is cooked to remove the raw taste of the flour. For a white roux we are careful not to let the butter brown in the pan; a brown roux is deliberately browned.

A liquid, usually stock or milk, is added to the roux. The real creativity and variety come with the addition of herbs, spices and other flavorings. Once you are familiar with the fundamental steps of French sauce-making, you can combine and experiment to create new sauces of your own.

White Sauces: The basic ones are Béchamel, made with milk; and Velouté, made with white stock. Both begin with a white roux.

BECHAMEL SAUCE   White Sauce with Milk
(Makes 2 cups)

3 tablespoons butter	2 cups milk
3 tablespoons flour	1 teaspoon salt

⅛ teaspoon white pepper

Melt the butter over moderate heat in a small heavy saucepan. Remove from heat and stir in the flour, using a whisk or wooden spoon, until well blended. Return to heat for one minute, stirring constantly. Don't let it brown. Remove from heat and slowly stir in the milk. When blended, return to heat once more and stir constantly until the sauce comes to a boil. Boil ½ minute and add salt and pepper. Serve with egg, cheese, poultry, fish or vegetable dishes.

VARIATIONS ON A BECHAMEL SAUCE

MORNAY SAUCE   Cheese Béchamel

Grate ½ cup Swiss or Parmesan cheese into 2 cups

45

Béchamel sauce, and heat gently until cheese melts. Do not boil. Serve with eggs, fish, poultry, veal, vegetables or noodles.

SAUCE AURORE   Tomato Béchamel

Stir 4 tablespoons tomato purée into two cups Béchamel sauce and simmer until well blended. Serve with eggs, fish, chicken or vegetables.

VELOUTE SAUCE   White Sauce with Stock
(Makes 2 cups)

3 tablespoons butter	1 teaspoon salt
3 tablespoons flour	⅛ teaspoon white pepper
2 cups white chicken	
stock *or* bouillon	

Melt butter in a small heavy saucepan over moderate heat. Remove from heat and add the flour, stirring with a whisk or wooden spoon. Cook one minute, stirring constantly. Don't let the flour brown. Remove from heat and stir in the stock until blended. Return to heat and cook until sauce thickens to the consistency of light syrup. Add salt and pepper. Serve with egg, poultry, cheese or vegetable dishes.

VARIATIONS ON A VELOUTE SAUCE

SAUCE AUX CAPRES   Caper Sauce

Heat 2 cups Velouté sauce and blend in 2 tablespoons capers and ¼ cup butter. Serve with fish, eggs or vegetables.

46

SAUCE CHIVRY White Wine Sauce

Simmer 1 tablespoon *each* dried tarragon and dried chervil with 1 cup white cooking wine for 15 minutes. Strain into 2 cups hot Velouté Sauce. Serve with eggs, fish or vegetables.

MORE WHITE SAUCE VARIATIONS

To make your sauces richer, you can add ½ cup heavy cream to the Béchamel; it becomes a Sauce Créme. Add the cream to the Velouté; you have a Sauce Suprème. Add any of the white sauces to a dish of eggs, vegetables, chicken or fish; sprinkle it with grated cheese, brown it under the broiler, and out comes a Gratiné.

What to do if something goes wrong:

If the Sauce Is Lumpy: This has probably happened because the roux was not well blended with the liquid. Strain it through a fine sieve, or put it in the electric blender for 30 seconds. No more lumps.

If the Sauce Is Too Thick: Simmer it, adding small amounts of milk or stock until you like the consistency.

If the Sauce Is Too Thin: Simmer the sauce over moderate heat, stirring constantly until the right consistency has been reached.

ABOUT BROWN SAUCES

The two basic ones to know are Sauce Brune and Sauce Espagnole. The major difference between them is the addition of tomato paste to Sauce Espagnole, which takes longer to cook. Otherwise they can be used interchangeably. Both can be refrigerated and kept indefinitely if boiled once a week. In an emergency, you can substitute canned beef gravy for either sauce (as indicated in the Convenience Food Table on page 179). Adding your own ingredients to the gravy, as suggested in the variations, will help to improve the flavor.

SAUCE BRUNE   Basic Brown Sauce
Makes 1¾ cups)

¼ cup butter
6 tablespoons flour

2 cups brown stock
1 teaspoon salt
¼ teaspoon pepper

Melt the butter in a small saucepan. Remove from heat and, using a whisk or wooden spoon, stir in the flour, blending thoroughly. Cook over moderate heat, stirring constantly, until the roux is nut brown (but don't burn the flour).

Remove from heat and slowly stir in the stock. Return to the heat and keep stirring for 3 minutes or until the sauce has thickened. Add salt and pepper to taste. Serve with beef, lamb or veal.

SAUCE ESPAGNOLE   Classic Brown Sauce
(Makes 3 cups)

¼ cup butter
½ cup onion, minced
½ cup carrots, minced
2 tablespoons parsley,
    minced

½ bay leaf
4 tablespoons flour
3 cups brown stock (p. 42)
1 tablespoon tomato paste
1 teaspoon salt
¼ teaspoon pepper

Melt the butter in a medium saucepan. Add the onion,

carrots, parsley and bay leaf. Cook, stirring frequently, over moderate heat for 10 minutes or until vegetables begin to brown.

Remove from heat and blend in the flour. Continue cooking until the mixture turns light brown, stirring occasionally, but be careful not to let it stick or burn. Stir in the stock and simmer 30 minutes.

Add the tomato paste, blending well, and season to taste with salt and pepper. Serve with beef or lamb.

VARIATIONS ON SAUCE BRUNE AND SAUCE ESPAGNOLE

SAUCE MADERE Brown Madeira Sauce
(Makes 1½ cups)

Cook rapidly 1½ cups Sauce Brune until reduced to about 1 cup. Stir in ½ cup wine, Madeira or cooking sherry. Heat, but don't boil. Serve with beef, veal, ham or poultry.

SAUCE AUX CHAMPIGNONS Mushroom Sauce
(Makes 1½ cups)

Sauté ½ cup thinly sliced fresh mushrooms or chopped canned mushrooms (well drained) in 1 tablespoon butter or margarine for 5 minutes. Drain and add to 1 cup heated Sauce Brune. Serve with chicken, eggs, fish, roast meats or casseroles.

SAUCE TOMATE Tomato Sauce
(Makes 2½ cups)

This is related to the brown sauce family, but it is beautifully red and thick and has a much longer cooking time. Although it may be used on spaghetti, you will find a true Italian spaghetti sauce on page 131. If you don't have time to make a proper Tomato Sauce, you can get by using canned tomato sauce instead, especially with the variations.

¼ cup carrots, finely diced	3 cups canned tomatoes
¼ cup celery, finely diced	1¼ cups brown stock
¼ cup onion, finely diced	½ teaspoon salt
¼ cup salad oil	Dash of pepper
2 tablespoons flour	½ teaspoon sugar
¼ teaspoon garlic powder	½ bay leaf

Cook the carrots, celery and onions in the oil in a small saucepan over moderate heat until the vegetables are tender but not brown, about 20 minutes.

Remove from heat and stir in the flour. Return to the heat and cook, stirring constantly, until flour is lightly browned. Add the garlic powder, tomatoes, brown stock, salt, pepper, sugar and bay leaf.

Bring the sauce to a boil and simmer gently for 1 hour, stirring frequently to keep it from sticking. The sauce will have thickened and been reduced by one half. Strain through a fine sieve, add salt and pepper to taste, and serve with shrimp, veal, chicken, meat loaf, noodles or zucchini.

VARIATIONS ON SAUCE TOMATE

Add one or more of the following 15 minutes before the sauce is finished.

2 teaspoons dried oregano	½ cup diced cooked shrimp
½ lb. browned ground chuck	½ cup canned minced clams, drained
½ can chopped mushrooms, drained	

BUTTER SAUCES

Butter is probably the single most characteristic ele-

ment in French cooking; not only as a fat, but as a flavoring in its own right. It makes an admirable sauce, with or without the addition of other flavorings. Butter sauces also happen to be easiest of all to prepare. They're well worth adding to your repertoire. Margarine may be substituted.

BEURRE NOISETTE   Brown Butter Sauce

Melt ¼ cup butter over moderate heat until it is a light brown. Serve on fish and hot vegetables.

BEURRE AUX FINES HERBES   Herb Butter Sauce

Melt ¼ cup butter and add *one* of the following herb combinations:

¼ teaspoon dried rosemary and 1 teaspoon chopped fresh (or ¼ teaspoon dried) parsley; or

¼ teaspoon dried tarragon and 1 tablespoon chopped fresh (or 1 teaspoon dried) parsley; or

2 tablespoons fresh chopped watercress and 1 teaspoon fresh (or ¼ teaspoon dried) parsley.

Serve on steak, poached fish, cauliflower or hot French bread slices.

BEURRE AMANDINE   Almond Butter Sauce

Sauté 3 tablespoons slivered almonds in ½ cup melted butter over moderate heat until almonds are golden brown. Serve with fish or green beans.

BEURRE BERCY   Butter in White Wine

Cook 4 minced shallots (or 1 teaspoon minced white onion) in ½ cup dry white cooking wine until all but 1 tablespoon of wine has evaporated. Blend in ½ cup melted butter. Add salt and pepper to taste. Serve on hamburgers or fish.

EGG-BASED SAUCES:
HOLLANDAISE AND MAYONNAISE

Once upon a time, making Hollandaise or Mayonnaise presented a challenge even to accomplished cooks; they required skill. Today they require skill or an electric blender. In the case of Mayonnaise, we think the blender method is by far the best. For Hollandaise, however, we think both methods are worth knowing.

True, blender Hollandaise is faster and easier than Classical. But perfectionists prefer the texture of Classical Hollandaise; and this method offers the serious cooking student the opportunity to learn many valuable secrets of French cooking. On the other hand, if you are faint of heart or short of time, you will find the blender Hollandaise offers sensational results for minimal efforts. However you make it, Hollandaise is a magnificent sauce to present at the table. Rich and delicate, it is a triumphant topping for poached fish or eggs, crabmeat, asparagus or broccoli. It can be kept warm in a double boiler (over *warm,* not hot, water) for an hour.

Do's and Don'ts for a Classical Hollandaise:

Do have the eggs at room temperature.

Do heat the eggs slowly, over low heat.

Do add the butter slowly.

Don't allow the water to boil.

Don't allow the sauce to boil or it will separate and the eggs will scramble.

CLASSICAL HOLLANDAISE   Double Boiler Method
(Makes 1½ cups)

¾ cup butter

3 egg yolks

1 tablespoon lemon juice

⅛ teaspoon salt

Bring 1½ cups of water to a simmer in the bottom of a double boiler. Meanwhile, melt all but 1 tablespoon of the butter in a small saucepan and let it cool.

Place the eggs yolks, lemon juice and salt in the top of the double boiler and mix well with a whisk or slotted spoon.

Add the remaining tablespoon of butter to the egg mixture and place on top of the gently simmering water. Stir constantly about ½ minute until the yolks begin to thicken.

Slowly pour the cooled melted butter into the sauce, while stirring briskly. The sauce is now thick and ready to serve. Remove double boiler from heat. *Serve warm, not hot.*

What to do if something goes wrong:

If the Sauce Is Too Thick: Whisk in 2 tablespoons of hot water or milk.

If the Sauce Is Too Thin: Lemon juice is the trick to know. Add 1 teaspoon of it to ¼ cup of the sauce, then slowly add the rest of the sauce, and it will thicken.

If the Sauce Separates: Add a tablespoon of cream and beat vigorously. This may or may not work, but it's worth trying.

If the Eggs Scramble Due to Too High a Heat: Start all over; it's a disaster.

QUICK HOLLANDAISE   Blender Method
(Makes ⅔ cup)

3 egg yolks   ¼ teaspoon salt
1 tablespoon lemon juice   ½ cup butter, melted

Place the egg yolks, lemon juice and salt in the blender jar. Cover and blend at high speed for 10 seconds. Remove cover, and with the blender at low speed, pour the butter into the sauce in a steady stream. Turn off the motor when all the butter has been added.

VARIATIONS ON HOLLANDAISE SAUCE

SAUCE MOUSSELINE
Hollandaise with Whipped Cream

Fold ½ cup chilled whipped cream into 1½ cups Hollandaise. Serve with fish, vegetables or soufflés (but not dessert soufflés).

SAUCE MALTAISE   Orange Hollandaise

Add 2 tablespoons orange juice to the egg yolks before you make the Hollandaise. This is particularly good with asparagus.

SAUCE BERNAISE   Tarragon Hollandaise

Add 1 tablespoon tarragon vinegar, ¼ teaspoon dried tarragon, ¼ teaspoon dried chervil and 1 teaspoon fresh parsley to ¾ cup Hollandaise. If you can possibly use fresh herbs, do so, substituting 1 teaspoon fresh for ¼ teaspoon dried. This famous sauce is superb on broiled steak or veal chops, as well as fish.

SAUCE MAYONNAISE
(Makes 1¼ cups)

Homemade Mayonnaise is so good you can serve it with pride on something as humble as a hard-cooked egg, which becomes an Oeuf à la Russe. Since it takes all of a minute to make in the blender, perfect Mayonnaise is within easy reach of all.

2 eggs	1 tablespoon lemon juice
¼ teaspoon dry mustard	or vinegar
½ teaspoon salt	1 cup salad oil

Place the eggs, mustard and salt in the blender container, cover, and blend at high speed for 20 seconds. Add the lemon juice or vinegar and blend 15 seconds more. Still blending at high speed, remove the cover and add the oil in a slow, steady stream. Taste, and add additional salt if necessary.

This Mayonnaise can be stored 6 days in the refrigerator.

VARIATIONS ON MAYONNAISE

Commercial mayonnaise may be substituted in these variations.

SAUCE REMOULADE   Herbed Mayonnaise

To 1 cup Mayonnaise add 2 tablespoons prepared mustard, 1 tablespoon *each* finely chopped parsley, celery, capers and pickle; ¼ teaspoon *each* dried tarragon and dried chervil; and 1 mashed anchovy. Serve chilled on fish, seafood or egg salads.

ROQUEFORT MAYONNAISE

To 1 cup Mayonnaise add ½ cup crumbled Roquefort (Bleu cheese may be substituted) and ½ cup dairy sour cream. Serve with fruits, celery or potato salad.

SAUCE PIQUANTE   Garlic-Mustard Mayonnaise

To 1 cup Mayonnaise add ¼ teaspoon dry mustard, ¼ teaspoon garlic powder, and 2 teaspoons instant minced onion (moistened according to label directions). Serve with cold shrimps or mussels, egg salad or deviled eggs or tuna.

OIL AND VINEGAR SAUCES

This category includes the basic French salad dressing, Sauce Vinaigrette, and its variations. Don't limit them to leafy salads alone; they are a wonderful way to serve almost any cold cooked vegetable (fresh or canned), including asparagus, broccoli, cauliflower, beets, green beans and chick-peas. Salad dressings taste best when they are freshly made, but they can be stored at room temperature for 2 or 3 days.

SAUCE VINAIGRETTE   Basic French Dressing

(Makes ½ cup)

2 tablespoons wine vinegar	¼ teaspoon salt
	⅛ teaspoon black pepper
6 tablespoons light olive oil or salad oil	¼ teaspoon dry mustard (optional)

Place all ingredients in a tightly covered jar and shake vigorously until well blended.

VARIATIONS ON SAUCE VINAIGRETTE

HERB VINAIGRETTE

To basic Vinaigrette add 1 teaspoon *each* fresh chopped parsley, tarragon, chives, thyme and basil (or ¼ teaspoon dried).

SAUCE RAVIGOTE

To Herbed Vinaigrette add ½ teaspoon *each* minced capers and minced scallions. Nice with cold meats as well as vegetables.

VINAIGRETTE NICOISE

As this is quite salty, prepare ½ cup basic Vinaigrette without salt and add 1 teaspoon *each* chopped anchovies, green olives and capers, plus ¼ teaspoon garlic powder (or 1 small clove crushed garlic).

HOW TO STAGE A LUNCH-IN

CHAPTER V

Here we present menus as well as recipes in the likelihood that sooner or later you may be called upon to give a luncheon. As a social ritual, the luncheon is more likely to happen to girls than to boys, but there is no hard rule about it. Luncheons (or suppers; the food is interchangeable) can be built around bridge or birthday parties, club meetings, religious groups and eventually, perhaps, bridal showers.

Luncheon food is lighter, less formal and usually cheaper than dinner food. It can be cold (which beats standing over a hot stove), portable (as in picnics) and it relies more heavily on vegetables, cheese and seafood than it does on hot meats.

Many of the entrées in this chapter would serve admirably as appetizers (Hors d'Oeuvres Variés and Quiche

Lorraine), side dishes (Ratatouille, Salade Niçoise) or hearty snacks (Hamburger Stroganoff, Finger Sandwiches). You'll find many more luncheon ideas in the chapters on crêpes and eggs; nothing, for example, surpasses a soufflé accompanied with a salad and rolls for lunch.

Recipes are given for the starred items in the menus. Each menu is followed by a timetable to give you some idea of when to do what.

MENU I

Tomates Farcies*
Concombres Vinaigrette*
Pomme à la Créme*

Mushroom-Stuffed
   Tomatoes*
Cucumbers Vinaigrette*
Apple Cream*

TOMATES FARCIES Mushroom-Stuffed Tomatoes
(Makes 6 servings)

3 firm medium tomatoes
½ pound fresh or 1 can
   (8 oz.) chopped mush-
   rooms
2 tablespoons butter or
   margarine

4 tablespoons onion,
   chopped
Dash of nutmeg
½ teaspoon salt
Dash of pepper
½ cup fresh breadcrumbs

Pre-heat oven to 350° F. Cut the tomatoes in half. Scoop out the pulp with a teaspoon. Save the pulp for a spaghetti sauce. Sprinkle salt and pepper on the insides of the tomatoes and place them, cut side down, on a paper towel to drain for 20 minutes.

Wipe fresh mushrooms with a damp sponge and chop fine; or drain canned mushrooms.

Melt butter in a small skillet, add onion and brown lightly. Add mushrooms, nutmeg, salt and pepper and stir until the mushrooms are soft, about 10 minutes over moderate heat.

Transfer tomatoes to a lightly oiled cookie sheet, fill with mushroom mixture, sprinkle with breadcrumbs and dot with additional butter. Bake 15 to 20 minutes or until the tops are brown.

To Serve: Arrange tomatoes on a platter garnished with canned mushroom caps and sprigs of parsley.

CONCOMBRES VINAIGRETTE
Cucumbers Vinaigrette
(Makes 6 servings)

2 tablespoons vinegar	½ teaspoon salt
6 tablespoons salad oil	¼ teaspoon pepper
1 tablespoon fresh *or* 1 teaspoon dried dill	1 cucumber, thinly sliced

Combine the vinegar, salad oil and dill. Add salt and pepper. Pour the sauce over the sliced cucumber and let stand at least two hours. Add additional salt and pepper if desired.

POMME A LA CREME   Apple Cream
(Makes 6 servings)

1 cup heavy cream	1 teaspoon vanilla
1 tablespoon confectioners' sugar	2 cups (15 oz. jar) apple sauce
1 teaspoon cinnamon	

Whip the cream with the sugar until it holds soft peaks. Fold in the vanilla, apple sauce and cinnamon. Serve chilled.

To Serve: Spoon into dessert dishes and garnish with thin strips of orange peel and candied violets (available from gourmet food shops).

WHAT TO DO WHEN

The Day Before: Prepare tomatoes for filling, cover and refrigerate. Make fresh bread crumbs. Prepare Cucumbers Vinaigrette completely and refrigerate.

The Same Day: One hour before lunch, remove cucumbers from the refrigerator. Complete Mushroom-Stuffed Tomatoes and bake. While the tomatoes are baking, prepare and garnish the Apple Cream.

MENU II

Jus de Tomate Piquante*   Tomato Juice Piquante*
Croque Monsieur*   French Toasted Ham and
Mousse des Fraises*   Cheese Sandwiches*
                           Strawberry Mousse*

JUS DE TOMATE PIQUANTE

Tomato Juice Piquante

(Makes 6 servings)

1 quart chilled tomato juice

2 teaspoons Worcestershire sauce

2 drops Tabasco

2 tablespoons lemon juice

1 teaspoon celery salt

Combine all ingredients in a large pitcher with a few ice cubes; stir vigorously. Taste and add more celery salt if necessary; be lavish with it, that's the kicker.

Remove the ice cubes and serve well chilled.

CROQUE MONSIEUR
French Toasted Ham and Cheese Sandwiches
(Makes 6 servings)

¾ cup butter or margarine
12 thin slices white bread
6 thin slices cooked ham

6 thin slices Gruyère or Swiss cheese
2 eggs, beaten
3 tablespoons milk

Use half the butter to spread on one side of each slice of bread after removing the crusts. Make six sandwiches using 1 slice each of the ham and cheese for each sandwich. Be sure the buttered sides of the bread are inside.

Beat the milk and eggs together. Cut the sandwiches in half and dip in the egg-milk mixture.

Melt remaining butter in a large skillet and sauté the sandwich halves over medium heat until golden brown on both sides. Serve hot.

To Serve: Garnish with ripe olives and sprigs of watercress.

MOUSSE DES FRAISES   Strawberry Mousse
(Makes 6 servings)

2 cups fresh strawberries, sliced *or* 2 packages (10 oz. each) frozen sliced strawberries, thawed

¾ cup sugar
1½ teaspoons vanilla
Dash of salt
1 cup heavy cream, whipped

Wash and hull the fresh strawberries. Put fresh or frozen strawberries in the blender for 30 seconds until puréed, or force through a fine sieve.

Mix the purée in a bowl with the sugar, vanilla and salt. Fold in the whipped cream. Refrigerate in a pretty serving bowl for at least 2 hours. Allow to stand at room temperature for 20 minutes before serving.

To Serve: Garnish with whole strawberries placed in concentric circles on top of the mousse.

WHAT TO DO WHEN

The Day Before: Prepare and refrigerate the ungarnished Strawberry Mousse.

The Same Day: Fifty minutes before lunch, prepare and refrigerate Tomato Juice Piquante. Remove Strawberry Mousse from refrigerator and garnish. Prepare and sauté the Croque Monsieur.

MENU III

Potage St. Germain*	Split Pea Soup*
Pain Chaud	Hot Crusty French Bread
Crêpes Framboise (p. 19)	Raspberry Crêpes (p. 19)

POTAGE ST. GERMAIN Split Pea Soup
(Makes 6 to 8 servings)

This is a thick, hearty pea soup, full of meat, vegetables and flavor. Since it's a one-pot recipe that can be made several days in advance (or longer, if you freeze it) it's an easy dish to serve to guests.

1 package (1 lb.) dried split peas, green or yellow
3 medium carrots
3 stalks celery
1 medium onion
4 sprigs parsley *or* 2 teaspoons dried parsley flakes

3 medium leeks *or* 6 green onions
4 beef soup bones (about 1 lb.)
½ lb. soup meat (chuck or short ribs)
1 ham hock
2 tablespoons salt
1 teaspoon pepper

4 quarts water

Wash the peas by putting them in a strainer and letting cool water run through them for several minutes. Slice the carrots, celery and onion in 1″ pieces. Chop the fresh parsley. Wash the leeks, being careful to remove all the dirt from the green ends.

Place all the vegetables, including the peas, in a large kettle (about 8-quart size) along with the bones, soup meat, ham hock, salt and pepper. Add water and bring to a boil.

Remove the white foam that forms on top of the water with a spoon, and simmer the soup over medium heat for 2 hours. The consistency of the soup should be a medium thickness, like a thick milk shake. If it's too thin, cook rapidly until it thickens.

Strain the soup into another kettle. Cut the meat into bite-sized pieces and return to the strained soup. Add additional salt and pepper if necessary.

To Serve: Spoon hot from a tureen into soup bowls and serve with hot French bread. Buy a package of small brown and serve French loaves and follow label directions for heating.

WHAT TO DO WHEN

The Day Before: Prepare and cook the Split Pea Soup. While the soup is cooking, prepare and make the crêpes but do not fill them. Refrigerate both the soup and the crêpes.

The Same Day: Forty-five minutes before lunch, reheat the Split Pea Soup. If it is too thick, thin with a little water, stirring well. While the soup is heating, warm the French bread in the oven. Prepare the banana filling for the crêpes, fill and keep warm in a moderate (350° F.) oven.

MENU IV

Bifteck Haché*	Hamburger Stroganoff*
Haricots Verts Vinaigrette*	Green Beans Vinaigrette*
Mousse au Chocolat (p. 170)	Chocolate Mousse (p. 170)

BIFTECK HACHE   Hamburger Stroganoff
(Makes 6 servings)

½ cup butter or margarine
½ cup onion, minced
1 pound ground beef
¼ teaspoon garlic powder
2 tablespoons flour
2 teaspoons salt
¼ teaspoon white pepper
¼ teaspoon paprika

1 cup sliced mushrooms, canned or fresh
1 cup canned cream of chicken soup, undiluted
1 cup dairy sour cream
6 hard rolls

Melt butter in a large skillet. Sauté onion until soft and golden. Stir in ground beef, garlic powder, flour, salt, pepper, paprika and mushrooms. Sauté, stirring occasionally, just until the beef is lightly browned.

Add the soup and simmer, uncovered, 10 minutes, stirring constantly. Add sour cream and blend well.

Cut a circle from the top of the rolls and hollow out the centers. Fill with the Stroganoff mixture.

To Serve: Place Hamburger Stroganoff on a large platter and garnish with sprigs of dill or parsley.

HARICOTS VERTS VINAIGRETTE
Green Beans Vinaigrette
(Makes 6 servings)

1 can (1 lb.) whole green beans, drained
1 jar (4 oz.) sliced pimiento
½ cup Sauce Vinaigrette (p. 57)

Place the green beans on an attractive serving dish. Arrange the pimiento over the beans and spoon the Sauce Vinaigrette on top. Allow to stand overnight in the refrigerator, but serve at room temperature.

WHAT TO DO WHEN

The Day Before: Prepare the Green Beans Vinaigrette and the Chocolate Mousse and refrigerate.

The Same Day: Thirty minutes before lunch, prepare and cook the Hamburger Stroganoff. Remove the beans and mousse from the refrigerator. Garnish the mousse. Just before serving, fill the rolls with the Stroganoff mixture.

MENU V

Quiche Lorraine*	Bacon and Cheese Tart*
Salade Verte*	Tossed Green Salad*
Orangines (p. 159)	Orange Wafers (p. 159)

QUICHE LORRAINE   Cheese and Bacon Tart
(Makes 6 to 8 servings)

Quiche Lorraine is a hot cheese custard pie flavored with bacon and sautéed onion. It is an excellent, all-purpose party food. Serve it as a hot hors d'oeuvre, cut into small pieces, as a midnight supper or take it on a picnic and eat it cold.

1 plain pie crust, 10″ (p. 162)	4 eggs, lightly beaten
	2 cups light cream
1 cup thinly sliced onion	½ teaspoon salt
1 tablespoon salad oil	¼ teaspoon ground nut-
1 cup grated Swiss cheese	meg
6 strips bacon, cooked crisp, drained and crumbled	¼ teaspoon white pepper

Preheat the oven to 400° F. Bake the pie shell for 8

67

minutes and set aside. Increase oven temperature to 450° F.

In a skillet, cook onions in oil until limp and yellow. Cover the bottom of the pie crust with grated Swiss cheese, onion and crumbled bacon. Combine the eggs, cream, salt and seasonings and pour over the cheese, bacon and onion.

Bake at 450° F. for 10 minutes. Reduce heat to 350° F. and bake 20 minutes more or until a knife or cake tester inserted in the center comes out clean.

Serve at once, slicing at the table into pie-shaped wedges.

SALADE VERTE   Tossed Green Salad
(Makes 6 servings)

1 medium head lettuce	1 cucumber, peeled and
½ cup Vinaigrette Niçoise	thinly sliced
Dressing (p. 57)	1 cup cherry tomatoes
1 small purple onion,	½ cup prepared garlic
thinly sliced	croutons

½ cup grated Parmesan cheese

Wash and drain the lettuce, patting each leaf dry with a paper towel. Tear into pieces and toss with the dressing in a salad bowl.

To Serve: Separate the onion slices into rings and arrange over the lettuce along with cucumber, tomatoes and croutons. Sprinkle with cheese.

WHAT TO DO WHEN

The Day Before: Bake the Orange Wafers and pie crust. Cover both and store at room temperature. Make the salad dressing.

The Same Day: One hour before lunch, prepare the Quiche Lorraine and bake. While ·the quiche is baking, prepare and toss the salad. Arrange and garnish the Orange Wafers.

MENU VI

Ananas Glace*

Suprème de Volaille
  Parmesan*

Salade d'Epinard

Crême Caramel (p. 165)

Pineapple Icebergs*

Breast of Chicken
  Parmesan*

Spinach and Bacon Salad*

Caramel Custard (p. 165)

ANANAS GLACE   Pineapple Icebergs
(Makes 6 servings)

Crushed ice

1 can (8 oz.) pineapple
  spears

1 can (20 oz.) pineapple
  juice

1 jar (8 oz.) cranberry
  juice

Put a little crushed ice into individual juice glasses and stand a pineapple spear upright in the ice in each glass. Combine the pineapple and cranberry juices and fill each glass.

SUPREME DE VOLAILLE PARMESAN
                    Breast of Chicken Parmesan
(Makes 6 servings)

½ cup flour

¼ teaspoon ground nut-
  meg

½ teaspoon salt

¼ teaspoon pepper

2 eggs, lightly beaten

½ cup fresh breadcrumbs

¾ cup grated Parmesan
  cheese

3 whole chicken breasts,
  boned and split in half

½ cup butter or margarine

69

Preheat the oven to 350° F. Season the flour with nutmeg, salt and pepper in one bowl. Beat the eggs in a second bowl. Mix the breadcrumbs and cheese in a third bowl.

Dredge each half chicken breast in the flour mixture, then in the eggs and finally in the breadcrumb mixture.

Melt the butter in a large skillet until foamy, and brown chicken on both sides. Transfer the chicken to an oven-proof dish and bake for 15 minutes or until tender.

To Serve: Garnish with lemon wedges, radish roses and parsley or watercress.

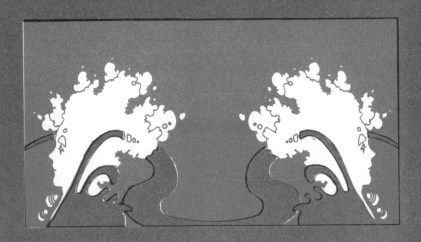

SALADE D'EPINARD   Spinach and Bacon Salad
(Makes 6 servings)

People who hate spinach are surprised at how good it tastes when prepared this way.

8 strips bacon
1 package (10 oz.) fresh
   spinach

½ cup Sauce Vinaigrette
   (p. 57)

Sauté the bacon until crisp and drain well on paper

towels. Wash the spinach, remove the stems and tear the leaves into large pieces. Drain well.

In a salad bowl, crumble the bacon onto the spinach and toss with Sauce Vinaigrette.

WHAT TO DO WHEN

The Day Before: Bake and refrigerate the Caramel Custard. Prepare the Sauce Vinaigrette. Grate the Parmesan cheese.

The Same Day: One hour before lunch, bake the chicken. While the chicken is baking, prepare the Pineapple Icebergs and the Spinach and Bacon Salad. Unmold and garnish the Caramel Custard.

MENU VII

Salade Niçoise*	Salade Niçoise*
Pain aux Fines Herbes*	Herb Bread*
Soufflé a la Vanille (p. 38)	Vanilla Soufflé (p. 38)

SALADE NICOISE

(Makes 6 servings)

This is a tangy mixture of cold vegetables and tuna, spiced with olives and anchovies. The whole is somehow more satisfying than the sum of its parts. Try it as a filler for a hero sandwich on a picnic and also as an extra dish on a cold buffet table.

Dressing:

½ cup salad or olive oil	1 clove garlic, crushed
2 tablespoons wine vinegar	1 teaspoon prepared mustard
½ teaspoon salt	¼ teaspoon black pepper

Combine all ingredients in a jar, cover and shake until thoroughly blended. Set aside.

71

Salad:

1 small head lettuce
1 can (7 oz.) tuna, drained
2 medium potatoes, boiled,
  peeled and sliced
1 green pepper, seeded
  and cut in rings
1 cup cooked green beans
1 can (2 oz.) flat anchovies
4 hard-cooked eggs,
  quartered

4 medium tomatoes,
  quartered
12 pitted black olives
1 small onion, chopped
1 tablespoon *each*
  chopped fresh tar-
  ragon, chives and
  parsley *or* ½ teaspoon
  each of the dried
  herbs

Separate the lettuce into leaves. Wash, drain well on paper towels and line a large salad bowl with them. Crumble the tuna and arrange it attractively over the lettuce along with the potatoes, green pepper, green beans, anchovies, eggs, tomatoes and olives.

Drizzle the chopped onion and herbs over the salad. Shake the dressing again, add it to the salad and toss at the table.

PAIN AUX FINES HERBES   Herb Bread
(Makes 6 to 8 servings)

1 large loaf French bread
½ cup butter or margarine,
  melted

¼ teaspoon   *each*   dried
  thyme, dill and tarra-
  gon
¼ cup grated Parmesan
  cheese

Preheat the oven to 350° F. Cut the bread in 1″ slices without cutting all the way to the bottom. Combine the herbs with the melted butter and mix well.

Brush both sides of each slice with the butter mixture. Sprinkle the top of the loaf with the grated cheese, and brush with remaining butter mixture.

Wrap the bread in foil, leaving the top open, and

bake for 20 minutes or until the top is lightly browned.

Serve the hot bread in a bread basket lined with a paper doily or cloth napkin.

WHAT TO DO WHEN

The Day Before: Prepare the base for the Vanilla Soufflé, reserving the egg whites. Make the salad dressing and refrigerate it. Prepare the bread, wrap in foil and refrigerate that, too.

The Same Day: Forty-five minutes before lunch, preheat the oven for the Vanilla Soufflé, remove egg whites and bread from the refrigerator. Place the bread in the oven to warm. Prepare and toss the salad.

Just before sitting down to eat, complete the soufflé and bake it while you are eating.

MENU VIII

Mousse aux Fruits de Mer*
Asperges Ravigote*
Profiteroles au Chocolat
  (p. 160)

Crab Mousse*
Asparagus Ravigote*
Profiteroles with Chocolate
  Sauce (p. 160)

MOUSSE AUX FRUITS DE MER   Crab Mousse
(Makes 6 to 8 servings)

2 tablespoons unflavored
  gelatin
2 cups cold water
6 tablespoons dried pea
  soup mix
1 teaspoon dry mustard

1 package (8 oz.) cream
  cheese, softened
3 drops Tabasco
2 tablespoons lemon juice
2 cups dairy sour cream
2 cans (6½ oz. each) crabmeat, drained

In a saucepan, sprinkle gelatin over water and let stand to soften. Add dried soup mix and mustard. Cook over moderate heat, stirring constantly, for 3 minutes. Pour hot mixture onto cream cheese and mix well. Add Tabasco, lemon juice and sour cream and beat until smooth.

Fold in the crabmeat. Be sure to remove any cartilage from the crabmeat first. Pour into a 2-quart mold (one in the shape of a fish is nicest) and refrigerate overnight.

To unmold, place the mold in 1 inch of lukewarm water for a minute, and run a sharp knife around the edge. Turn it upside down on a flat platter or tray.

To Serve: Arrange alternating slices of lemon and pimiento around the mousse.

ASPERGES RAVIGOTE Asparagus Ravigote
(Makes 6 servings)

1 can (1 lb.) asparagus 2 medium tomatoes
spears, drained ½ cup Sauce Ravigote
(p. 57)

Place asparagus spears over tomatoes sliced in ½"
circles on a serving dish. Spoon Sauce Ravigote over
the spears and allow to marinate for at least 2 hours.
Serve at room temperature.

WHAT TO DO WHEN

The Day Before: Prepare and refrigerate the Crab
  Mousse. Prepare the Sauce Ravigote. Bake the
  profiteroles. When they've cooled to room temperature, cover tightly. Make the Chocolate Sauce.
The Same Day: Two hours before lunch, prepare the
  salad and refrigerate it. Thirty minutes before lunch,
  fill the profiteroles and arrange them on a platter.
  Remove the mousse from the refrigerator, unmold
  and garnish. Place Chocolate Sauce in a serving
  dish.

MENU IX

Crudités* Raw Vegetable Dip*
Canapés Variés* Open-Faced Finger Sand-
Parfait aux Framboises* wiches*
  Raspberry Parfait*

CRUDITES Raw Vegetable Dip

On a large platter, arrange a selection of raw vegetables such as cauliflowerettes, carrot sticks and cucumber spears, radishes, cherry tomatoes and green

pepper slices. Serve with the following Sour Cream Sauce to use as a dip:

2 cups dairy sour
   cream
2 teaspoons onion,
   minced

Dash *each* garlic powder,
   salt, and pepper
¼ teaspoon *each* dried
   parsley and chives

Mix all ingredients and serve, chilled, in a bowl surrounded by the vegetables.

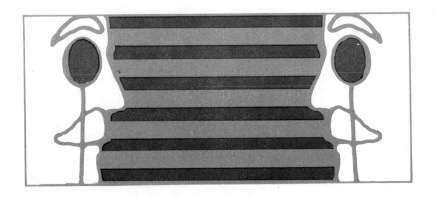

CANAPES VARIES   Open-Faced Finger Sandwiches
(Makes 16 Canapés)

Off-beat combinations and lots of variety are the keys to festive canapés. Each of the following recipes begins with:

4 slices white bread

2 tablespoons whipped or
   softened butter

Remove the crusts from the bread, spread with butter and cut each slice into fourths in either fingers or triangles. Top with any of the following fillings. If you like, you can make Herb Butter by adding a pinch of dried parsley and a pinch of tarragon. Arrange the finished canapés on a platter, cover with wax paper and a damp towel and refrigerate until a half hour before serving. Garnish the platter with a variety of olives.

Egg-Anchovy Canapés
(Makes 16 canapés)

4 hard-cooked eggs
¼ teaspoon paprika
1 can (2 oz.) rolled anchovies, drained
Dash white pepper
3 tablespoons mayonnaise

Mash eggs with paprika, pepper and mayonnaise. Spread on prepared bread and top each canapé with a rolled anchovy.

Cucumber-Sardine Canapés
(Makes about 16 canapés)

4 slices Swiss cheese, cut in fourths
2 small tomatoes, thinly sliced
1 unpeeled cucumber, thinly sliced
1 can (4 oz.) sardines, drained

Top each slice of prepared bread with slices of cheese, tomato, cucumber and a sardine.

Artichoke Canapés
(Makes about 16 canapés)

1 jar (6 oz.) marinated artichoke hearts, drained
1 jar (4 oz.) pimiento, sliced

Top each prepared slice of bread with one artichoke heart and garnish with a slice of pimiento.

77

Curried Tuna Canapés

(Makes about 16 canapés)

1 can (7 oz.) tuna, drained ¼ teaspoon curry powder
2 tablespoons mayonnaise 1 teaspoon salt
1 teaspoon lemon juice ½ teaspoon pepper
Watercress for garnish

Combine the tuna, mayonnaise, lemon juice and curry powder. Mix well. Add salt and pepper; taste and add additional salt and pepper if necessary. Spread on prepared bread and garnish with watercress.

Ham Canapés

(Makes about 16 canapés)

2 tablespoons prepared 4 to 6 slices cooked ham
  mustard 8 pitted ripe olives

Spread prepared bread with mustard and a slice of ham cut to fit. Top with half of a ripe olive. Tongue, turkey or chicken may be substituted for the ham.

PARFAIT AUX FRAMBOISES Raspberry Parfait

(Makes 6 to 8 servings)

2 cans (16 oz. each) sliced 2 packages (10 oz. each)
  cling peaches, drained.   frozen raspberries,
                             thawed
1 cup heavy cream, whipped

In a deep glass bowl, cover peaches with raspberries. Serve with a side dish of whipped cream.

WHAT TO DO WHEN

The Day Before: Prepare raw vegetables, cover and

refrigerate. Prepare and refrigerate Sour Cream Sauce and Herb Butter for canapés. Hard-cook eggs for sandwiches.

The Same Day: Two hours before lunch, remove Herb Butter and hard-cooked eggs from the refrigerator. Thaw raspberries.

One and a half hours before lunch, prepare Raspberry Parfait. Whip the cream and refrigerate it.

Prepare and garnish the sandwiches; cover with a damp towel until ready to serve.

Arrange vegetable platter; place dressing in a serving dish.

MENU X

Ratatouille*   Ratatouille*
Pain à l'Ail*   Garlic Bread*
Crème Brulée (p. 168)   Caramel Custard (p. 168)

RATATOUILLE   Ratatouille
(Makes 6 to 8 servings)

· A colorful mélange of vegetables cooked in garlic and oil, this dish may be served hot or cold.

1 medium eggplant, peeled if desired	¼ cup olive oil
	1 large onion, thinly sliced
3 small zucchini squash	
3 medium tomatoes *or*	3 cloves garlic, minced
1 can (1 lb.) Italian plum tomatoes, drained	2 green peppers, seeded and cut in rings
	1½ teaspoons salt
	½ teaspoon pepper

Slice the eggplant, zucchini and fresh tomatoes ¼"

79

thick. Heat ⅛ cup of the oil in a heavy casserole for 3 minutes and add one clove of minced garlic, plus some of the eggplant, onion, green pepper, zucchini and tomatoes. Sprinkle with salt and pepper. This becomes one layer of vegetables.

Add the second clove of minced garlic and make a second layer of vegetables over the first; sprinkle with salt and pepper.

Continue layering until all the vegetables have been used. Add the remaining ⅛ cup oil to the top of the last layer, plus more salt and pepper.

Cover and simmer over moderate heat for 30 to 35 minutes, or until the vegetables are tender. The mixture should be thick, so pour off excess liquid if necessary. Gently stir two or three times and add additional salt and pepper if needed.

PAIN A L'AIL   Garlic Bread
(Makes 6 to 8 servings)

1 large loaf French bread
½ cup butter or margarine, melted

3 cloves garlic, crushed
¼ teaspoon paprika

Preheat oven to 350° F. Make slices in the bread about 1 inch apart, cutting only about ¾ of the way to the bottom. Add the garlic to the melted butter, mix well and brush both sides of each slice with the mixture. Dust the top of the loaf with paprika.

Wrap the bread in foil, leaving the top open. Brown in the oven for 15 minutes. Garlic Bread can be prepared in advance and refrigerated. Reheat in a warm oven just before serving.

WHAT TO DO WHEN

The Day Before: Prepare Ratatouille, cool to room temperature and refrigerate. While the Ratatouille is cooking, prepare and refrigerate the Garlic Bread. Make the Caramel Custard and refrigerate.

The Same Day: One and a half hours before lunch, unmold the Caramel Custard and replace in the refrigerator. Thirty minutes before lunch, remove Ratatouille from refrigerator (heat if desired) and warm the Garlic Bread in the oven.

MENU XI

Pamplemousse Grillée*   Broiled Grapefruit*
Jambalaya aux Crevettes*   Shrimp Jambalaya*
Crème Bavaroise au   Coffee Bavarian Cream
  Café (p. 169)   (p. 169)

PAMPLEMOUSSE GRILLEE Broiled Grapefruit
(Makes 6 servings)

3 medium grapefruit,   6 teaspoons light brown
  halved and sectioned   sugar
    6 green glacé cherries

Preheat the broiler. Cut a thin slice from the rounded bottom of each grapefruit half to give it a flat base on which to stand. Place the grapefruit on an ungreased cookie sheet.

Sprinkle the halves with brown sugar and broil 5 to 7 minutes or until golden brown and bubbly.

Garnish each half with a glacé cherry and serve immediately.

JAMBALAYA AUX CREVETTES   Shrimp Jambalaya
(Makes 6 servings)

This is a famous example of the French influence on the Creole cooking of Louisiana, a cuisine which also reflects Spanish and Indian influences. Jambalaya can be cooked the day before, refrigerated and reneated just before serving. It is a good choice for buffet suppers, too.

2 tablespoons olive or
  salad oil
2 medium onions, minced
1 clove garlic, crushed *or*
  1 teaspoon garlic
  powder
1 small green pepper,
  minced
2 pounds raw shrimp,
  shelled and deveined

1 cup uncooked rice
1 can (1 lb.) tomatoes
2 cups chicken stock or
  bouillon
1 bay leaf
1 teaspoon salt
Dash pepper
1 teaspoon sugar
½ cup grated Parmesan
  cheese

2 teaspoons fresh parsley, chopped

Preheat oven to 350° F. Heat the oil in a large skillet. Add the onion, garlic and green pepper. Cook 5 minutes until onions are golden.

Add shrimp and continue to cook over moderate heat until the shrimp turn pink, about 3 to 5 minutes. Transfer the shrimp mixture to an oven-proof serving dish and set aside.

To the same skillet, add the rice, cooking and stirring constantly until it is light brown. Add the tomatoes, chicken stock, seasonings and sugar. Cover and simmer until the rice is tender and the liquid is absorbed, about 20 minutes.

Add the rice to the shrimp and mix gently. Add additional salt and pepper to taste. Sprinkle the top with Parmesan cheese and heat in a 350° oven for 10 minutes. Sprinkle with parsley and serve.

If the Shrimp Jambalaya has been refrigerated, bring to room temperature and increase oven time to 25 minutes.

WHAT TO DO WHEN

The Day Before: Prepare and cook Jambalaya, cool to room temperature and refrigerate. While the Jambalaya is cooking, make the Bavarian Cream. Refrigerate it.

The Same Day: Forty-five minutes before lunch, remove the Jambalaya from the refrigerator. Preheat oven. Preheat the broiler; prepare the Broiled Grapefruit. Heat the Jambalaya in the oven. Unmold and garnish the Bavarian Cream. Ten minutes before lunch grill the grapefruit.

MENU XII

Bifteck Haché au Vin
  Rouge*
Pommes Frites*
Maçédoine de Fruits*

Hamburgers in Red Wine*
French Fried Potatoes*
Fruits in Liqueur*

BIFTECK HACHE AU VIN ROUGE

Hamburgers in Red Wine

(Makes 6 servings)

2 pounds ground round
  or lean chuck
1 medium onion, minced
¾ cup catsup
½ cup packaged dried
  breadcrumbs

2 eggs
1 teaspoon salt
¼ teaspoon black pepper
½ cup beef stock or
  bouillon
½ cup red cooking wine

Preheat oven to 375° F. Place the ground beef,

onion, ½ cup of the catsup, breadcrumbs, eggs, salt and pepper in a bowl. Mix thoroughly.

Shape the meat mixture into 6 oval patties, each about ¾" thick. Arrange on a baking dish and spread each patty with the remaining catsup. Bake 35 minutes.

Transfer the patties to a serving platter and keep warm. Skim off and discard any fat in the baking dish, but keep the juices.

Add the bouillon and red wine to the juices in the dish and stir over medium heat 2 to 3 minutes, scraping up the browned bits in the dish. Season with additional salt and pepper, if necessary.

To Serve: Place the hamburgers on a platter, spoon the wine sauce over them, and garnish with cherry tomatoes and watercress or parsley.

POMMES FRITES   French Fried Potatoes
(Makes 6 servings)

4 medium potatoes, peeled   Oil for frying
Salt to taste

Cut the potatoes into very thin slices and then into narrow strips about ¼" thick. Cover with cold water at least one hour.

Heat the oil (enough to cover the potatoes) in a deep fryer or a large skillet. The oil is hot enough when one potato stick dropped into it rises immediately to the surface, surrounded by bubbles.

Fry the potatoes 6 to 7 minutes. Remove and drain on paper towels.

Just before serving, re-heat the oil and fry the potatoes rapidly for 3 minutes, until crisp and brown. Drain well and serve sprinkled with salt.

MACEDOINE DE FRUITS   Fruits in Liqueur
(Makes 6 servings)

1 package (10 oz.) frozen sliced peaches, thawed

1 package (10 oz.) frozen sliced strawberries, thawed

1 package (10 oz.) frozen melon balls, thawed

3 tablespoons cherry liqueur *or* orange liqueur *or* brandy

Place the fruit in a serving bowl and sprinkle with the liqueur. One teaspoon orange extract may be substituted for the liqueur. Spoon into individual dishes at the table. If desired, garnish each serving with shredded coconut.

WHAT TO DO WHEN

The Day Before: Peel and slice the potatoes, cover with water and refrigerate.

The Same Day: Two hours before lunch, defrost the frozen fruits. One hour before lunch, prepare the hamburgers. While they are baking, prepare and refrigerate the Fruits in Liqueur. Fry the potatoes. Just before serving, garnish the platters.

FRENCH FEASTS

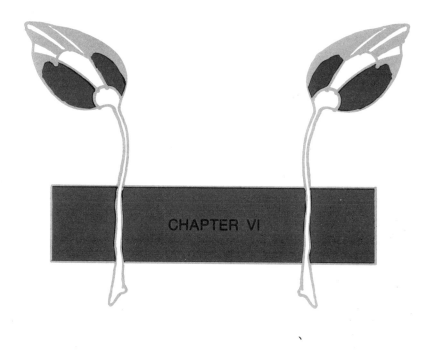

CHAPTER VI

In this chapter, you'll find not just great dinner menus and recipes, but a fund of French cooking lore besides. By the time you've worked your way through the ten main courses, you will know a great deal about most basic methods of cooking meat, fish and poultry. You will also have the skill to tackle new recipes with confidence, or to improvise first-rate dishes of your own.

All desserts and other recipes not marked with an asterisk can be found on the indicated pages.

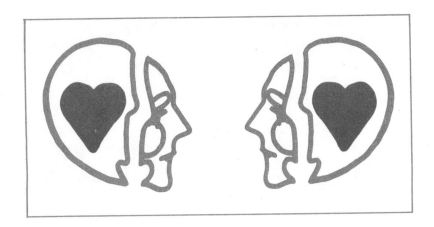

MENU I

Gouda Farci*	Gouda Surprise*
Gigot d'Agneau à la · Boulangère*	Roast Leg of Lamb Boulangère*
Petit Pois*	French Peas*
Salade d'Ananas*	Pineapple Salad*
Crêpes Jubilee (p. 21)	Jubilee Crêpes (p. 21)

GOUDA FARCI Gouda Surprise

(Makes 6 servings)

1 Gouda cheese (7 to 9 oz.)	2 cloves garlic, crushed
½ cup beer	1 package (3 oz.) cream cheese, softened
1 teaspoon prepared mustard	1 tablespoon caraway seeds
Dash nutmeg	

Cut a 2″ circle in the top of the Gouda and scoop out the cheese, using a grapefruit knife or a teaspoon. Leave a shell about ¼″ thick plus the red skin of the cheese.

Shred the cheese. Place half the beer and half the Gouda cheese in an electric blender along with the mustard, nutmeg and garlic. Blend 30 seconds.

Add the remaining beer and Gouda cheese and blend until smooth. Add the cream cheese and blend 30 seconds more.

Transfer the mixture to a small bowl and mix in the caraway seeds. Fill the Gouda shell with the mixture. Refrigerate, covered, until 1 hour before serving.

To Serve: Sprinkle the top with additional caraway seeds. Serve with a butter knife on a round platter surrounded with an assortment of crackers.

GIGOT D'AGNEAU A LA BOULANGERE

Roast Leg of Lamb

(Makes 6 servings)

The lamb roasts on a bed of sliced onions and potatoes, and is delicious. The French method of roasting meat is to sear it at a high temperature to seal in the juices, then to lower the temperature until the meat is cooked. French lamb is usually served slightly pink inside. You may substitute a boned 3-pound loin of pork, but be sure in that case to increase the cooking time to 2 hours at 350° F.

1 leg of lamb, about 6 pounds	1 teaspoon pepper
	4 large potatoes
1½ teaspoons salt	3 medium onions
½ cup butter or margarine	

Preheat the oven to 400° F. Rub the lamb with salt and pepper. Place in a roasting pan and brown in the oven, uncovered, for 30 minutes.

While the lamb is browning, peel the potatoes and onions and slice in ¼" rounds.

Melt the butter in a large casserole over medium

heat. Dry the vegetables with paper towels if they are damp, and cook them in the casserole about 20 minutes or until they are limp. Season with an additional 2 teaspoons of salt.

Remove the lamb from the oven and place in the casserole on top of the vegetables. Reduce oven to 375° F. and roast, uncovered, 1 hour for medium rare lamb.

To Serve: Carve the lamb right in the casserole over the vegetables at the table.

PETITS POIS   French Peas
(Makes 6 servings)

1 can (1 lb.) miniature sweet peas	Dash of white pepper
½ cup butter or margarine	1 small head Boston lettuce
1 tablespoon sugar	4 sprigs fresh parsley
Dash of salt	1 can (8 oz.) onions, drained

Drain the sweet peas, reserving ½ cup liquid. Combine the liquid from the peas, 6 tablespoons of the butter, sugar, salt and pepper in a small saucepan and bring to a boil.

Stir until the butter has melted. Add the lettuce, cut in ½" circles, and the parsley sprigs tied together.

Simmer, covered, 10 minutes.

Add the peas and onions and cook, covered, another 20 minutes. Add additional salt and pepper if necessary. Discard the parsley. Add remaining butter, stirring gently until absorbed.

To Serve: Garnish with sprigs of mint.

SALADE D'ANANAS Pineapple Salad

(Makes 6 servings)

1 small head Boston
   lettuce
2 cans (1 lb. each) sliced
   pineapple, drained

1 can (1 lb.) orange
   sections, drained
1 package (8 oz.) cream
   cheese at room tem-
   perature

1 package (2¾ oz.) chopped walnuts

Separate the head of lettuce into leaves, wash and drain. Arrange a few leaves on individual salad plates, and top each with 2 slices of pineapple surrounded by orange sections.

Form 12 cream cheese balls by rolling about a teaspoonful of the cheese between your hands. Roll each ball in the chopped nuts and place one in the center of the pineapple rings on each serving.

WHAT TO DO WHEN

The Day Before: Prepare the Crêpe batter; let stand while making the Gouda Suprise and the Pineapple Salad. Refrigerate the cheese, tightly covered, and the salad, also tightly covered.

Peel and slice the potatoes and onions for the Roast Lamb, place in cold water to cover and refrigerate.

Make the crêpes, cover and refrigerate. Prepare the sauce for the Crêpes Jubilee, cover and refrigerate.

The Same Day: An hour and forty-five minutes before dinner, prepare the lamb and place in the oven.

Remove the Gouda Surprise from the refrigerator and garnish.

Prepare and cook the French Peas.

Remove the salad, crêpes and Jubilee sauce from the refrigerator. Get the ice cream, serving dish and liqueur ready for the crêpes; heat the sauce.

Artichauts Piquant*
Poulet à l'Orange*
Riz au Safran*
Tarte aux Pommes (p. 164)

Spicy Artichokes*
Chicken with Orange
    Sauce*
Saffron Rice*
French Apple Tart (p. 164)

ARTICHAUTS PIQUANT Spicy Artichokes
(Makes 6 servings)

1 medium green pepper,
    minced
1 medium onion, minced
2 stalks celery, minced
2 cloves garlic, crushed
½ cup olive or salad oil
2 medium tomatoes,
    diced
1 pimiento, diced
¼ cup dry white cooking
    wine

Juice of 1 lemon
1 teaspoon salt
¼ teaspoon pepper
1 head Boston lettuce
1 can (1 lb.) artichoke
    hearts, drained
2 tablespoons chopped
    fresh parsley
1 hard-cooked egg,
    chopped
1 lemon, cut in wedges

In a medium saucepan, cook the green pepper, onion, celery and garlic in oil over medium heat until wilted, about 5 minutes. Add the tomatoes, pimiento, wine, lemon juice, salt and pepper. Cook 5 minutes more, cool for 15 minutes.

To Serve: Arrange the lettuce leaves on a serving platter with the artichokes on top. Spoon the marinade over the artichokes, and garnish with the parsley, egg and lemon wedges.

POULET A L'ORANGE Chicken with Orange Sauce
(Makes 6 to 8 servings)

The same basic roasting instructions may be followed in roasting a turkey or any other poultry; only the roasting time will vary according to the size of the bird.

2 whole broiler-fryer
chickens, 2½ to 3
pounds each
1 teaspoon salt
6 tablespoons softened butter or margarine

1 cup diced onions
1 cup diced carrots
2 tablespoons salad oil
mixed with 3 tablespoons melted butter or margarine

Preheat the oven to 425° F. Wash and dry the chickens and sprinkle the insides with salt. Rub the inside and outside with the softened butter. Place on a rack in a shallow roasting pan, breast up. Surround the chickens with the onions and carrots and roast, uncovered, 15 minutes or until lightly browned.

Reduce heat to 350° F., turn the chickens on their sides, and baste with the oil and butter mixture. Continue to baste every 10 minutes; this makes the skin crisp and keeps the birds from drying out.

Halfway through the roasting time (about ¾ of an hour) turn the chickens on their other sides. After 1½ hours, test for doneness by gently piercing the drumstick with a fork. If the juices run clear, not pink, the chickens are done.

Cut them in quarters and transfer them to a warm serving dish. They can be kept in the turned-off oven for 30 minutes.

Orange Sauce:

¼ cup red wine vinegar
½ cup white cooking wine
½ cup sugar
2 tablespoons currant
    jelly

2 oranges
2 cups Brown Sauce
    (p. 48) or canned
    chicken gravy
3 tablespoons orange
    liqueur

Cook the vinegar, wine and sugar in a small heavy saucepan over high heat, stirring constantly with a wooden spoon, until the mixture reaches a golden caramel color (310° to 338° F. on a candy thermometer).

Add the currant jelly and cook over moderate heat until well blended.

Meanwhile, peel and section the oranges. Cut the peel into thin strips, place in a saucepan with just enough water to cover them and bring to a boil. Drain off the liquid from the orange peel.

Add the Brown Sauce or chicken gravy and the orange liqueur to the currant jelly mixture and heat.

To Serve: Spoon half the sauce over the chicken pieces, arrange the orange peel and sections over them, garnish the platter with watercress. Serve the rest of the sauce in a sauceboat.

RIZ AU SAFRAN   Saffron Rice

(Makes 6 servings)

2 tablespoons minced
  onion
5 tablespoons butter or
  margarine
1 cup rice
¼ teaspoon dried
  crumbled saffron

½ teaspoon salt
Dash of pepper
2 cups chicken stock or
  bouillon
½ cup grated Parmesan
  cheese

Sauté the onion in 1 tablespoon of butter in a medium saucepan over medium heat until the onion is golden.

Blend in the rice with 2 more tablespoons of butter. Cook, stirring constantly, until the rice is dry and just begins to stick to the pan.

Add the saffron, salt, pepper and stock. Bring to a boil, stir thoroughly once and simmer, covered, for 20 minutes until the liquid is absorbed. Dot with remaining butter and sprinkle with Parmesan cheese.

WHAT TO DO WHEN

The Day Before: Prepare artichokes, cover and refrigerate. Prepare and partially bake the tart shell, cool and wrap tightly.

Cook the Orange Sauce for the chicken, cool to room temperature, cover and refrigerate.

Season the applesauce for the tart. Grate Parmesan cheese.

The Same Day: Prepare and roast the chicken. Fill and bake the tart. Prepare and cook the Saffron Rice. Remove the artichokes from the refrigerator. Heat the Orange Sauce.

MENU III

Champignons Farcis*	Stuffed Mushrooms*
Boeuf à la Mode*	Braised Beef in Red Wine*
Salade Verte (p. 68)	Tossed Green Salad (p. 68)
Profiteroles au Chocolat (p. 161)	Profiteroles with Chocolate Sauce (p. 161)

CHAMPIGNONS FARCIS Stuffed Mushrooms

(Makes 6 servings)

18 large fresh mushrooms	¼ teaspoon black pepper
4 tablespoons olive or salad oil	3 tablespoons grated Parmesan cheese
½ cup minced onion	1 tablespoon dried pack-aged breadcrumbs
1 clove garlic, crushed	
½ medium green pepper, seeded and minced	2 tablespoons chopped capers (optional)

¼ cup dry white cooking wine

Preheat oven to 375° F. Wipe the mushrooms with a damp towel and dry. Remove the stems and chop fine, leaving the mushroom caps whole.

Heat 2 tablespoons of the oil in a skillet, sauté the onion, garlic and green pepper for 5 minutes. Add the chopped mushroom stems and cook 5 minutes more.

Combine the onion mixture with the remaining ingredients. Fill the mushroom caps with the mixture, place on an oiled jelly roll pan and sprinkle with the remaining 2 tablespoons of oil. Bake 15 minutes.

To Serve: Use a small glass to cut circles from foil. Shape the foil circles into little cups for the mushrooms. Serve hot.

BOEUF A LA MODE   Braised Beef in Red Wine
(Makes 6 to 8 servings)

This dish is marinated in wine, vegetables and seasonings before cooking. Then it is cooked in the marinade, which is used later in making the sauce.

In braising, the meat is first browned in hot fat, then cooked, covered, in liquid, either on top the stove or in the oven. You'll find it a useful method for cooking lamb and pork as well as beef.

The Marinade:

4 pounds rump, chuck or bottom round	2 medium carrots, sliced
	1 large onion, sliced
1½ teaspoons salt	1 bay leaf
¾ teaspoon pepper	3 tablespoons powdered
2 cups dry red cooking wine	thyme
	4 sprigs fresh parsley
½ cup brandy, optional	2 cloves garlic, halved

If possible, have the butcher lard the beef with salt pork and tie it securely. Rub the meat with salt and pepper, place in a large bowl and add all the remaining ingredients. Marinate at least 5 hours at room temperature, turning occasionally, or overnight in the refrigerator.

Braising the Beef:

4 tablespoons salad oil	4 cups Brown Stock (p. 42)
Marinade (above)	or beef bouillon

Preheat oven to 350° F. Remove the meat from the marinade and dry with a paper towel. Heat the oil in a large, burner-proof casserole over moderately high heat, and brown the meat on all sides.

Pour off the oil, add the marinade and the stock and bring to a boil. Cover and cook in the oven 3 hours or until tender. Transfer the meat to a serving platter, remove strings and keep warm while preparing the sauce.

The Sauce:

Liquid in which the meat   1 tablespoon cornstarch
   has cooked   3 tablespoons water

Strain the braising liquid through a fine sieve into a medium saucepan. Cook rapidly over high heat until the liquid is reduced by one-third; about 3½ cups remain.

Reduce heat to moderate. Combine the cornstarch and water in a small glass, add slowly to the liquid in the saucepan and stir with a whisk until lightly thickened. Add additional salt and pepper if necessary.

The Garnish:

2 cans (1 lb. each) baby   1 can (1 lb.) white onions,
   carrots, drained   drained
        3 tablespoons butter or margarine

Heat the carrots and onions in the butter in a medium saucepan over moderate heat for 5 minutes, turning gently with a wooden spoon.

Spoon a little of the sauce onto a large serving platter. Slice the beef and arrange overlapping slices down the center. Surround with the vegetables. Add sprigs of parsley at one end of the platter. Serve the remaining sauce in a sauceboat.

WHAT TO DO WHEN

The Day Before: Prepare the marinade and marinate the beef. Prepare and bake the profiteroles. When baked, cool and cover tightly. Make the Chocolate Sauce while the profiteroles are baking. Allow the sauce to cool to room temperature and refrigerate. Make the salad dressing.

Prepare the profiterole filling. Cover and refrigerate.

The Same Day: At least four hours and 15 minutes before dinner, remove the meat from the marinade; cook as directed.

One and a half hours before dinner, prepare the Stuffed Mushrooms. Wash the salad greens, dry and refrigerate.

Fill the profiteroles, place in the refrigerator. Put the sauce in a sauceboat.

Prepare the garnish for the Braised Beef in Red Wine; keep it warm.

Remove the beef from the oven; prepare the sauce. Toss the salad.

Place the Stuffed Mushrooms in the oven. Arrange the Braised Beef on a platter.

MENU IV

Bouillabaisse*   Bouillabaisse*
Pain Chaud   Hot French Bread
Soufflé au Chocolat (p. 39)   Chocolate Soufflé (p. 39)

BOUILLABAISSE Bouillabaisse
(Makes 6 servings)

Bouillabaisse is a savory stew combining a wide assortment of seafood flavored with wine and garlic. It has no English name and needs none. More than anything else, with the possible exception of the French national anthem, it is what makes Marseilles famous, for that is where it originated.

No two restaurants in the world serve the same version of Bouillabaisse, not even in Marseilles. It all depends upon what fish is available and on the whim of the chef. If you must substitute for some of the fish, or if you have any whims of your own that you'd like to express, feel free to do so; it's right in the spirit of Bouillabaisse.

It is essential to include bread in the menu for the purpose of sopping up the broth. All proper Frenchmen dunk rather than leave an excellent sauce on the plate; but a well-bred Frenchman dunks the bread with a fork rather than with his fingers.

Since fish is one of the least fattening foods available, it is appropriate to follow Bouillabaisse with a rich dessert such as the Chocolate Soufflé.

It is important to simmer the fish gently and to avoid overcooking or it will fall apart.

2 cups minced onions
1 clove garlic, minced
½ cup olive or salad oil
2 sprigs parsley
1 bay leaf
1 can (2 lbs., 12 oz.) plum tomatoes, drained
¼ teaspoon fennel seed
2 teaspoons salt
1 pound fresh red snapper

1 pound fresh flounder
1 pound haddock
2 pounds small lobster tails in the shells
1½ quarts water
¼ teaspoon crumbled saffron
1 teaspoon dried thyme
½ teaspoon black pepper
1 pound shrimp, shelled and deveined

1 cup dry white cooking wine

Cook the onions and garlic in the oil in a 6-quart kettle until transparent and golden, about 5 minutes. Add the parsley, bay leaf, tomatoes, fennel seed, salt, fish—sliced 1″ thick—lobster tails and water. Cover and bring to a boil.

Reduce heat and simmer gently for 15 minutes. Add the saffron, thyme, pepper, shrimp and wine and simmer 10 minutes more. Add additional salt and pepper if necessary.

To Serve: Spoon the fish into individual soup plates. Add a slice of French bread to each plate and pour the broth over the bread. Serve with grated Parmesan cheese.

WHAT TO DO WHEN

The Day Before: Prepare the soufflé base, cover and refrigerate. Refrigerate the unbeaten egg whites.

The Same Day: One hour before dinner, remove the soufflé base and the egg whites from the refrigerator.

Prepare the Bouillabaisse. Warm the French bread. Butter and sugar the soufflé dish. Just before sitting down at the table, finish the soufflé and let it bake during dinner.

MENU V

Paupiettes de Veau*	Stuffed Veal Scallops*
Nouilles Amandine*	Noodles with Almonds*
Courgettes Vinaigrette*	Zucchini Vinaigrette*
Fraises Romanoff (p. 171)	Strawberries Romanoff (p. 171)

PAUPIETTES DE VEAU Stuffed Veal Scallops
(Makes 6 servings)

Thin slices of veal are folded around a filling of ham, cheese and mushrooms, dipped in batter, sautéed until crisp and then baked with a sauce.

The key word here is sautéed, which means cooked lightly in a small amount of fat. When sautéing meat, the object is to get it browned and crisp on the outside

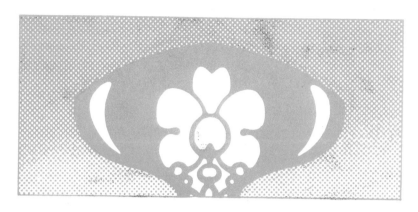

while sealing in the juices. To accomplish this, *the pieces of meat must not touch* each other in the pan. If they do, the meat will begin to stew and become tough and stringy.

½ pound fresh mush-
    rooms, chopped *or*
    1 can (8 oz.) chopped
    mushrooms, drained
1 medium onion, minced
3 tablespoons salad oil
6 veal scallops
6 slices Gruyère or Swiss
    cheese
6 thin slices cooked ham
2 eggs, slightly beaten
1 cup packaged dried
    breadcrumbs
1 cup flour

1 teaspoon salt
½ teaspoon pepper
⅓ cup oil
1¾ cups Brown Stock
    (p. 42) *or* beef
    bouillon
¼ cup dry white cooking
    wine
1 tablespoon tomato
    paste
1 tablespoon flour mixed
    with 3 tablespoons
    cold water
1 teaspoon dried tarragon

Sauté the fresh mushrooms and onion in 3 table-spoons oil until limp. Or add the drained canned mush-rooms to the onions when they're cooked. Add salt and pepper.

Cover each veal scallop—they should be pounded very thin until each one is about 6″ long and 3″ wide—with a slice of cheese and a slice of ham. Place a heaping tablespoon of the mushroom mixture in the middle of each scallop and fold in half, keeping the ham and cheese tucked inside the edges.

Press the edges of the veal together so the filling is sealed in. Dip each filled scallop first in the slightly beaten eggs, then the breadcrumbs, finally the flour seasoned with salt and pepper, coating well on both sides.

Heat the ⅓ cup oil in a large skillet until it is quite hot and sauté the scallops on both sides until golden brown. Transfer to an oven-proof serving dish.

Preheat the oven to 350° F. Pour off all the oil from the skillet and add the stock, wine, tomato paste, flour and water mixture and tarragon. Stir well over moderate heat, scraping up the browned bits in the skillet, until thickened, about 5 to 7 minutes.

Strain the sauce and spoon it over the veal scallops. Bake 25 minutes. If the sauce begins to brown before it is done, cover the dish with foil.

To Serve: Garnish with cooked mushroom caps and thin slices of lemon and arrange several sprigs of watercress at one end of the platter.

NOUILLES AMANDINE   Noodles with Almonds
(Makes 6 servings)

This should not be cooked in advance, but if you must hold them for a while before serving, add half the butter and keep the noodles warm in a covered double boiler. Add the rest of the butter, the parsley and almonds just before serving.

1 package (8 oz.) thin
    noodles
1 teaspoon salt
1 tablespoon salad oil
2 quarts boiling water
¼ cup butter, melted

1 package (2¾ oz.)
    blanched slivered
    almonds
2 tablespoons chopped
    fresh parsley

Add the noodles, salt and oil to 2 quarts of rapidly boiling water. Boil rapidly for 20 minutes and drain well.

Add the butter, almonds and parsley. Add additional salt and pepper if necessary. Stir gently and remove to a serving dish.

To Serve: Sprinkle slivered almonds and 1 tablespoon minced cooked ham over the noodles.

COURGETTES VINAIGRETTE   Zucchini Vinaigrette
(Makes 6 servings)

This slender green squash, known as marrows in England, is usually called by its Italian name, zucchini, in this country. In this recipe, it is served cold like a salad. It can be prepared well in advance and refrigerated until a half hour before serving time.

3 medium zucchini squash
1 teaspoon salt
2 tablespoons wine vinegar

2 tablespoons salad oil
¼ teaspoon salt
Dash of black pepper

1 small clove garlic, crushed

Scrub the zucchini and cut it into slices ¼" thick. Place it in enough rapidly boiling water to cover. Add 1 teaspoon salt and simmer 5 minutes. Drain well. The zucchini should be tender but not mushy.

Cool to room temperature.

Put the remaining ingredients in an empty jar, cover and shake well until thoroughly blended. Pour the dressing over the squash. Serve chilled.

To Serve: Overlap the zucchini slices on an oval platter. Garnish with cherry tomatoes or overlapping tomato slices.

WHAT TO DO WHEN

The Day Before: Hull the strawberries, but do not wash them. Prepare the Zucchini Vinaigrette completely.
The Same Day: Prepare the strawberries for the Strawberries Romanoff. Prepare and cook the Veal Scallops. Remove the zucchini from the refrigerator. Cook the noodles while the veal is baking.

MENU VI

Soupe à l'Oignon*	Onion Soup*
Poulet Grillé à l'Estragon*	Broiled Tarragon Chicken*
Pommes Duchesse*	Duchess Potatoes*
Salade de Tomate*	Tomato Salad*
Pêche Melba (p. 171)	Peach Melba (p. 171)

SOUPE A L'OIGNON   Onion Soup
(Makes 6 servings)

¼ cup butter or margarine
5 cups onions, thinly sliced
2 quarts beef stock or bouillon

1 teaspoon salt
½ teaspoon pepper
1 loaf French bread
½ cup grated Parmesan cheese

Melt the butter in a heavy medium saucepan. Cook the onions in the butter until they just begin to turn light brown.

Add the stock or bouillon, salt and pepper and bring to a boil. Reduce heat and simmer, covered, for 25 minutes. Add additional salt and pepper if necessary.

To Serve: Preheat broiler. Place a slice of French bread in each oven-proof soup bowl, add the soup. Sprinkle generously with grated Parmesan cheese and gratiné 4″ from the heat 3 minutes or until the cheese browns.

POULET GRILLE A L'ESTRAGON

Broiled Tarragon Chicken

(Makes 6 servings)

Broiling is the easiest way to cook chicken. It should not be broiled rapidly or it will burn on the outside and be undercooked inside, so keep it a respectable distance from the heat. The secret of broiling chicken so it is crisp and golden outside, moist and tender inside, is frequent basting with butter, oil, wine, stock or a combination of these. In this recipe, all of them plus tarragon are used for extra-special flavor.

4 tablespoons melted butter
4 tablespoons salad oil
2 tablespoons dried tarragon
1 teaspoon salt
Juice of 1 large lemon
¼ cup dry white cooking wine
2 broiler-fryer chickens (about 2½ lbs. each) cut in pieces

Preheat the broiler. Combine the butter, oil, tarragon, salt, lemon juice and wine.

Dry the chicken pieces with paper towels and coat each piece with the tarragon mixture.

Broil, skin sides down, about 6 inches from the heat for 20 minutes. Baste after 10 minutes.

Turn the chicken and broil another 20 minutes, basting halfway through the cooking time.

Transfer the cooked chicken to a warm serving platter. Add any remaining basting sauce to the pan juices, and heat, stirring and scraping up the browned bits in the pan. Spoon the sauce over the chicken.

To Serve: Garnish the chicken platter with lemon wedges and sprigs of fresh tarragon, if available, otherwise use watercress or parsley. Surround with Duchess Potatoes.

POMMES DUCHESSE   Duchess Potatoes
(Makes 6 servings)

6 medium potatoes, peeled
and thinly sliced
1 teaspoon salt

⅛ teaspoon white pepper
⅛ teaspoon nutmeg
1 whole egg plus 2 egg
yolks

Cook the potatoes in boiling water and salt until soft. Drain well.

Mash with a potato masher or force through a food mill. Add pepper, nutmeg and eggs; beat until fluffy with a wooden spoon or with an electric mixer.

Add additional salt and pepper if necessary.

Place the potato mixture in a pastry bag and pipe through a plain or rosette tip onto a lightly oiled jelly roll (shallow) pan, dividing the mixture into 6 servings. Or use a large spoon to mound the potatoes. Drizzle the top of each serving with melted butter and place in a moderate (350° F.) oven until lightly browned. Remove the finished potatoes with a pancake turner and place on the same platter with the Tarragon Chicken.

SALADE DE TOMATE   Tomato Salad
(Makes 6 servings)

2 large tomatoes
1 large Bermuda onion

¼ cup Vinaigrette sauce
(p. 57)

½ teaspoon dried oregano

Slice the tomatoes and onion very thin. Arrange the tomatoes on a platter with the onion rings on top. Spoon Vinaigrette sauce over the tomatoes and onions, sprinkle with oregano and chill until serving time.

WHAT TO DO WHEN

The Day Before: Prepare and cook Onion Soup. Cool to room temperature and refrigerate in individual soup bowls. *Do not gratiné.* Defrost raspberries.

While the soup is cooking, prepare the Tomato Salad and dressing. Refrigerate separately.

Prepare peaches and Melba sauce. Refrigerate separately.

Slice French bread for soup; cover tightly. Grate the Parmesan cheese.

The Same Day: Cook the potatoes and chicken. While the chicken is cooking, finish preparing the potatoes and pipe onto a shallow pan.

Remove the Onion Soup and Tomato Salad from the refrigerator. Spoon the Vinaigrette sauce over the tomatoes. *Don't forget to baste the chicken!*

Prepare the Peach Melba and refrigerate. Place the potatoes in the oven to brown. Gratiné the Onion Soup.

MENU VII

Coquille St. Jacques*	Scallops in the Shell*
Broccoli aux Anchois*	Broccoli with Anchovy But-
Petits Pains Chauds	ter*
Trifle Anglaise (p. 167)	Hot Rolls
	English Trifle (p. 167)

COQUILLE ST. JACQUES   Scallops in the Shell
(Makes 6 servings)

The scallops are poached in white wine, then combined with cream sauce in individual shells (or ramekins if you don't have shells) and gratinéed. In poaching shellfish, the liquid must be simmering, not boiling. Be very careful never to overcook any shellfish or it will toughen and turn rubbery. A "gratin" is literally a brown crust. In French cooking, a dish that is gratinéed always means it has been sprinkled with grated cheese (sometime breadcrumbs, too), dotted with butter and placed under the broiler for a few minutes until lightly browned.

2 pounds sea scallops, cut into quarters

5 tablespoons butter or margarine

1 cup dry white cooking wine

2 shallots, minced *or* 1 tablespoon minced onion

1½ cups Béchamel sauce (p. 45)

1 teaspoon salt

½ teaspoon pepper

⅓ cup fresh breadcrumbs

¼ cup grated Swiss cheese

Grease 6 scallop shells or ramekins with 1 tablespoon of the butter. Preheat the broiler.

Simmer the scallops, 2 tablespoons of butter, wine

and shallots or onion in a small saucepan for 8 minutes. Remove scallops. Strain the liquid and simmer 10 minutes longer.

Add the Béchamel sauce, scallops, salt and pepper. Spoon into the prepared shells, sprinkle with breadcrumbs and cheese, dot with remaining butter and gratiné under the broiler about 5 minutes or until warmed through, bubbly and browned.

To Serve: Place the shells or ramekins with the Coquille on paper doilies on individual serving dishes.

BROCCOLI AUX ANCHOIS
Broccoli with Anchovy Butter
(Makes 6 servings)

2 pounds fresh *or* 2 pkgs. (10 oz. each) frozen broccoli spears
2 teaspoons salt

½ cup butter, melted
2 teaspoons anchovy paste *or* 1 can (2 oz.) anchovies, mashed
1 teaspoon lemon juice

Wash fresh broccoli and cut off tough part of stems. Place in boiling salted water to cover and simmer, covered, for 8 to 10 minutes until broccoli is tender. Drain. If using frozen broccoli, follow package directions for cooking.

Combine the melted butter, anchovy paste and lemon juice and spoon over cooked broccoli.

To Serve: Place the broccoli in the center of an oval serving dish and surround it with 6 broiled tomatoes.

WHAT TO DO WHEN

The Day Before: Prepare Trifle and refrigerate. Wash

and trim fresh broccoli, dry and refrigerate. Grate Swiss cheese and prepare breadcrumbs. Prepare the Anchovy Butter and refrigerate.

The Same Day: Whip cream for the Trifle and refrigerate. Prepare the Coquille, spoon into shells and keep warm. Preheat the broiler. While scallops are simmering, cook broccoli, drain and place in an oven-proof dish. Warm butter sauce and spoon over broccoli. Keep warm in the oven.

Place rolls and broccoli in the oven to warm. Gratiné the Coquilles. Remove the Trifle from refrigerator before serving dinner.

MENU VIII

Beignet au Fromage*	Hot Cheese Fritters*
Daube de Porc*	Pork Braised in Wine*
Salade d'Epinard (p. 70)	Spinach Salad (p. 70)
Mousse au Chocolat (p. 170)	Chocolate Mousse (p. 170)

BEIGNET AU FROMAGE   Hot Cheese Fritters
(Makes about 24 small fritters)

These are a combination of Choux Paste (p. 160) and grated cheese, fried until golden brown. They are fluffy and crisp and great as hot hors d'oeuvres.

1 recipe Choux Paste (p. 160)	½ cup coarsely grated Gruyère or Swiss cheese
2 teaspoons salt	
1 teaspoon prepared mustard	6 tablespoons Parmesan cheese, grated
Dash of Cayenne pepper	Oil for frying

113

Prepare the Choux Paste and vigorously stir in the salt, mustard, pepper and cheeses. Season to taste, but be sparing with the Cayenne; it's hot. The paste should be quite sharp.

Heat 3 inches of oil in a large, deep skillet until it starts to bubble. Drop teaspoons of paste, one at a time, into the hot oil. Do not overcrowd the pan. Turn the beignets as they puff and brown. When crisp and golden, remove with a slotted spoon and drain on paper towels. Keep warm in a 300° F. oven until ready to serve.

To Serve: Place a bouquet of watercress in the center of a round serving dish and surround it with the Beignets. Sprinkle the Beignets with grated Gruyère cheese.

DAUBE DE PORC   Pork Braised in Wine
(Makes 6 servings)

A *daube* is any meat or vegetable that is braised in red wine and stock with herbs, spices and vegetables. In France it is cooked in a special casserole called a *daubière,* but any large, heavy casserole will do. This is a succulent meal-in-a-pot that can be cooked the day before and reheated. The important rule in cooking pork is *never undercook it.* Beef, lamb or chicken may be substituted for the pork in this recipe.

3 pounds shoulder of pork, boned and cubed
¼ cup flour
3 tablespoons salad oil
3 medium carrots, sliced
1 large onion, sliced
2 cloves garlic, crushed
¼ teaspoon black pepper
1 teaspoon salt

1 can (1 lb.) tomatoes, drained
2 cups dry red cooking wine
2 cups brown beef stock or bouillon
1 can (1 lb.) whole potatoes, drained
1 can (1 lb.) baby carrots, drained

1 tablespoon fresh parsley, minced

Preheat the oven to 350° F. Lightly dredge the cubes of pork in flour. Heat the oil in a roasting pan and brown the meat on all sides, a few pieces at a time, over moderately high heat. Do not overcrowd the pan. When browned, push the meat to one side and cook the carrots and onion until golden. Pour off the oil.

Add the garlic, pepper, salt, tomatoes, wine and bouillon to the meat in the casserole. Bring to a boil, cover, and braise in the oven for 1½ hours. Add the potatoes and cook 30 minutes longer. If necessary, season with additional salt to taste.

To Serve: Garnish with warmed baby carrots and the minced parsley.

WHAT TO DO WHEN

The Day Before: Fix Beignet batter and refrigerate. Prepare the greens for the Spinach Salad, dry and refrigerate. Prepare the salad dressing. Make the Chocolate Mousse and refrigerate it.

The Same Day: Two and a half hours before dinner, cook the Daube de Porc. Thirty minutes before dinner, deep fry the Beignets and keep warm in the oven. Assemble and toss the salad. Remove the mousse from the refrigerator and garnish.

MENU IX

Crevettes au Vin Blanc*	Shrimp in White Wine
Tournedos Chasseur*	Filet Steak with Mush-
Tomate Grillée*	rooms*
Crêpes Suzette (p. 23)	Broiled Tomatoes
	Crêpes Suzette (p. 23)

There are times in a person's life when one feels the need to produce a superlative dinner, a dinner of enormous elegance.

Here, we think, is a dinner that offers complete social security to the chef. It is the only dinner that requires last-minute cooking, but if you organize the work schedule the following way, it will go smoothly.

First, have all advance preparations made before you begin. About 20 minutes before the guests arrive, start grilling the tomatoes. As soon as the tomatoes are out

of the broiler, put in the shrimp, keeping the tomatoes warm in a 250° oven. When the shrimp are cooked, keep them warm in a chafing dish if you have one, or in the oven with the tomatoes in their own bake-and-serve dish.

When the guests arrive, serve the shrimp as a hot hors d'oeuvre in the living room, where a tray has been set up with small plates, forks and serving spoon. From there it will be easy for you to escape to the kitchen 15 minutes before you plan to serve the main course. There you will sauté the tournedos, which will be served as soon as they are done at the table along with the broiled tomatoes. The object of these maneuvers is to avoid disappearing for 15 minutes from the table. By having the first course in another room, your absence is perfectly acceptable.

CREVETTES AU VIN BLANC   Shrimp in White Wine
(Makes 6 servings)

30 medium shrimp (about 1½ lbs.)

½ cup dry white cooking wine

3 cloves garlic, crushed

½ cup butter, melted

1 teaspoon chopped parsley

Early in the day or the day before, peel and devein the shrimp. Cut a long slice, about ¼" deep, along the underside of each shrimp. Refrigerate until ready to cook.

Preheat the broiler. Place the shrimp, underside down, in an oven-proof serving dish. Combine the wine, garlic, butter and parsley, and spoon the mixture over the shrimp. Broil, 6" from the heat, for 7 to 10 minutes, until the shrimp are bright pink.

Serve the hot shrimp in the dish in which they were cooked. Garnish with lemon wedges.

TOURNEDOS CHASSEUR

Filet Steaks with Mushrooms
(Makes 6 servings)

The steaks will be sautéed quickly in very hot butter, searing the outsides and sealing in the juices. Why sauté instead of broil? Because the average oven broiler may let some of the juices escape to form steam; the result is partly steamed meat. As with all sautéed meats, the steaks should not touch in the pan. If you don't have a large enough skillet to prevent crowding, use two pans at once. In this recipe, the butter in which the steak is sautéed adds greatly to the flavor.

118

The recipe calls for fresh button (very small) mushrooms, if available. Always choose mushrooms that are white, with closed caps; the undersides of the caps should be firmly attached to the stems. All you have to do to clean such mushrooms is wipe the caps with a damp cloth. If the mushrooms are brown or dirty, rinse them very quickly in cold water, dry them immediately and cut off the brown tips of the stems. Mushrooms should be dry before sautéeing or they will not brown.

½ pound fresh button mushrooms *or* 1 can (8 oz.) mushrooms, drained
½ cup butter
6 filet steaks, 1″ thick

1 teaspoon salt
½ teaspoon pepper
½ cup beef stock or bouillon
1 can (2 oz.) liver pâte, optional

Earlier in the day, heat 2 tablespoons of butter in a large skillet and sauté the fresh mushrooms 5 minutes. Set aside.

Fifteen minutes before serving time, heat 6 tablespoons butter in a very large skillet until hot but not brown. While the butter is heating, season the filets with salt and pepper. Sauté 3 to 4 minutes on each side for medium rare steaks. Remove to a warmed platter.

Add the cooked or canned mushrooms and the stock to the skillet and cook 2 to 3 minutes, until hot. Spoon the mixture over the steaks and serve at once.

To Serve: Put a slice of live pâte on each steak, if desired. Surround the steaks with broiled tomatoes and garnish with watercress.

TOMATE GRILLEE   Broiled Tomatoes

(Makes 6 servings)

3 large firm tomatoes, cut in half

¼ cup butter or margarine, melted

6 tablespoons fresh breadcrumbs

3 tablespoons grated Parmesan cheese

Earlier in the day, cut a thin slice off the rounded ends of the tomato halves so they will stand without wobbling. Place on an ungreased cookie sheet, cut sides up.

Combine butter, breadcrumbs and cheese and spread evenly on top of the tomato halves.

Preheat the broiler. Broil the tomatoes 6" from the heat for 6 to 8 minutes, until lightly browned. They can be kept warm in a 250° F. oven until ready to serve.

WHAT TO DO WHEN

The Day Before: Peel, devein and refrigerate the shrimp. Prepare and cook the crêpes. Prepare the sauce for the crêpes. Grate cheese and prepare the breadcrumbs. Slice pâte for Tournedos and refrigerate.

The Same Day: Three hours before dinner, sauté mushrooms and set aside. Prepare tomatoes and place on cookie sheet. Prepare the shrimp butter sauce and set aside.

Remove the crêpes and sauce from the refrigerator and assemble the flambé utensils.

Thirty minutes before dinner, broil tomatoes and keep warm. Broil the shrimp and serve.

Twenty minutes after serving shrimp, sauté the Tournedos.

MENU X

Vichyssoise*   Cold Potato Leek Soup*
Veau Marengo*   Veal Marengo*
Nouilles au Beurre*   Buttered Noodles*
Pamplemousse en Gelée*   Grapefruit Salad Mold
Poire Hélène (p. 172)   Pear Parfait (p. 172)

VICHYSSOISE   Cold Potato Leek Soup
(Makes 6 to 8 servings)

This is probably the world's most popular cold creamed soup; but it can also be served hot. It is quickly made, especially with a blender.

6 cups chicken stock   4 leeks, white parts only,
    (p. 43) or bouillon   sliced
3 medium potatoes,   1 teaspoon salt
    peeled and sliced   1 cup light cream
        2 tablespoons chopped chives

Bring the stock to a boil in a medium saucepan and add the potatoes, leeks and salt. Simmer 35 to 40 minutes, until the vegetables are tender.

Remove from heat and blend until smooth in a blender, or force through a fine sieve. Add the cream and blend 10 seconds more. Season with additional salt, if necessary, and chill.

To Serve: Serve the Vichyssoise in individual chilled soup bowls with chopped chives sprinkled on top.

VEAU MARENGO   Veal Marengo
(Makes 6 servings)

This is a variation of a famous dish; a stew combining white wine, tomatoes, mushrooms and herbs. According to tradition, the original version was created with a stray hen caught by Napoleon's cook during the battle of Marengo in northern Italy. It is stewed on top of the stove in a large saucepan or heavy burner-proof casserole.

3 pounds shoulder of veal, cubed
1½ teaspoons salt
¾ teaspoon pepper
4 tablespoons salad oil
2 tablespoons flour
1 cup dry white cooking wine
2 cups beef stock or bouillon
1 clove garlic, crushed

1 can (1 lb.) tomatoes, drained
1 bay leaf
½ teaspoon powdered thyme
½ teaspoon dried tarragon
1 can (1 lb.) button mushrooms, drained
1 can (1 lb.) onions, drained
2 slices toasted white bread, quartered

Sprinkle the veal with salt and pepper. Heat the oil in a saucepan or casserole and brown the veal on all sides, a few pieces at a time. Remove the veal with a slotted spoon and set aside.

Add the flour to the oil and stir until golden brown and smooth. Blend in the wine and bouillon, loosening the browned bits at the bottom of the pan. Add the garlic, tomatoes, bay leaf, thyme, tarragon and veal and stir well. Cover and simmer 1 hour.

Add the mushrooms and onions and cook 15 minutes longer. Add additional salt and pepper if necessary.

To Serve: Top stew with toast points and sprinkle with parsley.

NOUILLES AU BEURRE   Buttered Noodles

Follow the recipe for Noodles Amandine (p. 104), omitting the almonds.

PAMPLEMOUSSE EN GELEE
Grapefruit Salad Mold
(Makes 6 servings)

1 can (1 lb.) grapefruit
  sections with liquid
1½ cups boiling water
1 package (3 oz.) lime-
  flavored gelatin
1 jar (4 oz.) maraschino
  cherries, drained
1 can (8 oz.) grapefruit
  sections, drained
1 jar (4 oz.) green glacé
  cherries

Drain the grapefruit sections, reserving ½ cup of the liquid, and set aside.

In a bowl, combine 1½ cups boiling water with the ½ cup grapefruit liquid and add to the lime-flavored gelatin. Stir until gelatin is dissolved and refrigerate until syrupy; about 30 to 45 minutes.

Gently fold the maraschino cherries and grapefruit sections into the gelatin and pour into a 3-cup mold. Chill until firm.

123

To Serve: Unmold the salad in the center of a serving dish. Place crisp lettuce leaves around the mold, and alternate additional grapefruit sections and glacé cherries on the lettuce. Note: To unmold the salad, run the tip of a sharp knife along the edge of the mold. Place the mold in 2 inches of warm water for 15 seconds and invert on a serving platter.

WHAT TO DO WHEN

The Day Before: Cook and refrigerate the Vichyssoise. While the soup is cooking, prepare and refrigerate the Grapefruit Salad Mold. While the gelatin is thickening, prepare chocolate sauce for the Pear Parfait.

The Same Day: An hour and a half before dinner, cook the veal. Forty minutes before dinner, boil water for noodles. While water is coming to a boil, unmold and garnish the Grapefruit Salad Mold. Cook noodles. While noodles are cooking, prepare and refrigerate the Pear Parfait. Drain and butter noodles. Arrange platters and serve dinner.

COOK'S TOUR OF THE WORLD

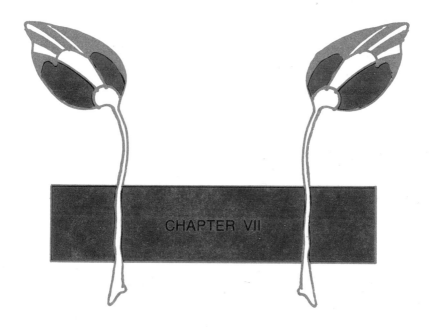

CHAPTER VII

Although France is the home of Grande Cuisine, it does not have exclusive rights to gourmet cooking. Great cuisines influence each other, often with surprising results. As northern Italian cooking influenced France when Catherine de Medici married Henri II, so Italian spaghetti began its career in China, under the name of *lo mein* noodles, and was introduced to Italy by Marco Polo.

Most of the dishes in this chapter can be eaten without a knife, which makes them excellent choices for lap service at large buffet dinners. The recipes can be doubled for a crowd.

MENU FROM GREECE

Greek cuisine resembles that of Armenia, Turkey and Syria, particularly in the frequent appearance of lamb in the main dish. Lemon and cinnamon are characteristic flavorings, and a typical Greek meal is likely to include their famous olives and feta, a cheese made from goat's milk.

Artichokes Piquant (p. 93)
Moussaka*
Athenian Salad*
Halva*

MOUSSAKA

(Makes 8 servings)

This hearty casserole combines ground lamb, eggplant, tomato and cheese. It can be cooked in advance and reheated in the oven.

4 tablespoons olive or
    salad oil
1 large onion, chopped
2 pounds ground lamb
2 cloves garlic, crushed
¼ teaspoon powdered
    thyme
¼ teaspoon dried rosemary
¼ teaspoon cinnamon
1 can (1 lb.) tomatoes,
    drained

1 lemon peel, grated
2 eggs, beaten
½ cup dried breadcrumbs
1½ teaspoons salt
¾ teaspoon pepper
3 medium eggplants
½ cup flour
    Oil for frying
1 cup Béchamel Sauce
    (p. 45)
½ cup grated Parmesan
    cheese

Heat the olive or salad oil in a large skillet; add onion and cook until soft and golden, about 5 minutes.

Add the lamb and cook over moderate heat, stirring occasionally, until lightly browned.

Mix in the garlic, thyme, rosemary, cinnamon, tomatoes, lemon peel, eggs, breadcrumbs, salt and pepper. Cook for 5 minutes and set aside.

Slice the unpeeled eggplants in ½" thick rounds and coat lightly with flour. Heat the frying oil (about 1" deep) in a large skillet and sauté the eggplant on both sides until golden brown. Drain on paper towels.

Preheat the oven to 350° F. Place the lamb mixture in a large shallow pan, cover with the eggplant slices, then the Béchamel Sauce. Sprinkle the Parmesan cheese on top and bake 45 minutes to 1 hour. Serve hot.

ATHENIAN SALAD
(Makes 6 to 8 servings)

¼ pound black Greek olives

1 large cucumber, thinly sliced

4 stalks celery, minced

2 green peppers, seeded and cut in rings

5 radishes, thinly sliced

3 medium tomatoes, cut in wedges

4 green onions, thinly sliced

6 tablespoons olive oil

2 tablespoons wine vinegar

¼ teaspoon oregano

¼ teaspoon black pepper

½ teaspoon salt

½ pound feta cheese, diced

Combine the olives, cucumber, celery, green pepper, radishes, tomatoes and green onions in a large salad bowl.

To Serve: For dressing, place the olive oil, vinegar, oregano, pepper and salt into a screw top jar and shake well. Toss the salad with the dressing and sprinkle the cheese on top.

HALVA

(Makes 6 to 8 servings)

¼ cup butter at room
  temperature
½ cup sugar
3 eggs
1 cup farina
½ teaspoon almond
  extract
2 tablespoons grated
  orange peel

¼ cup ground almonds
3 tablespoons orange
  juice
¾ cup honey
⅓ cup water
1 tablespoon lemon juice
2 tablespoons orange
  juice

Preheat the oven to 350° F. Grease an 8″ square baking pan.

Cream the butter; add the sugar slowly. Add the eggs, one at a time, beating constantly.

Stir in the farina, almond extract, orange peel, almonds and 3 tablespoons orange juice. Blend well and pour into the prepared cake pan. Bake 35 minutes or until a cake tester inserted in the center comes out dry. Cool cake thoroughly.

While cake cools, combine the honey, water, lemon and orange juices and simmer for 20 minutes in a saucepan. Spoon the warm syrup over the cooled cake. Cut in squares and serve.

WHAT TO DO WHEN

The Day Before: Prepare and refrigerate, covered, the salad vegetables, salad dressing, and the artichokes. Dice the cheese. Bake the cake.

The Same Day: Two hours before dinner, prepare the syrup for the cake. Prepare the Moussaka—although this can be made earlier and reheated 20 minutes before serving in a 375° F. oven. A half hour before dinner, pour the syrup over the cake. Remove artichokes from the refrigerator. Toss salad with dressing and sprinkle with cheese. Cut cake into squares and arrange on a cake plate.

MENU FROM ITALY

You are probably familiar enough with Italian food to recognize the combination of olive oil, tomatoes, cheese (usually Parmesan or Mozzarella) and especially oregano that finds its way into most Italian-American dishes. However, if you should ever find yourself partying at a palazzo in northern Italy, you can expect somewhat different fare. Most Italian cooking in this country represents southern Italy, but from Rome northward the cuisine becomes more varied and delicate, with less reliance on the tomato sauce to which we are accustomed. You will also find that in Italy, pasta (any macaroni product) is the course that comes after the anti-pasto (or appetizer) and before the main meat course. Italians prefer their pasta *al dente,* or slightly firm, so beware of over-cooking.

Antipasto*
Spaghetti with Meat Sauce*
Spinach Salad (p. 70)
Ricotta Cream Puffs*

ANTIPASTO

(Makes 6 servings)

2 cans (2 oz. each) rolled anchovies, drained
1 can (4⅜ oz.) boneless sardines, drained
1 jar (7 oz.) ripe olives
1 jar (6 oz.) marinated artichokes

2 bunches finocchio, cleaned and separated
2 jars (4 oz. each) whole pimientos, drained
½ pound thinly sliced prosciutto
1 bunch radishes
½ pound Italian salami, thinly sliced

Arrange all the ingredients on a large serving platter. Serve with cruets of olive oil, vinegar and a filled pepper mill. Let your guests help themselves.

SPAGHETTI WITH MEAT SAUCE
(Makes 6 to 8 servings)

¼ cup olive or salad oil
1 cup chopped onion
2 garlic cloves, crushed
1 pound ground chuck or
    round steak
2 cans (2 lbs. each) plum
    tomatoes
1 can (6 oz.) tomato paste

1 tablespoon sugar
1 bay leaf
1 teaspoon *each* dried
    basil and oregano
2 teaspoons salt
½ teaspoon pepper
1 pound spaghetti
Parmesan cheese

Heat the oil in a large saucepan. Add the onion and garlic and cook until limp, about 5 minutes. Add the ground meat and cook, stirring often, until the meat is browned lightly.

Add tomatoes, liquid and all, tomato paste, sugar and bay leaf. Simmer, covered, 1½ hours. Add the basil, oregano, salt and pepper and continue to simmer, uncovered, 20 minutes more, stirring occasionally. If sauce is too thick, add water, stir and simmer.

Cook the spaghetti according to the directions on the package. Pour the meat sauce over the drained spaghetti; sprinkle with grated Parmesan cheese.

Serve with Spinach Salad, omitting the bacon.

RICOTTA CREAM PUFFS
(Makes 6 servings)

1 recipe Choux Paste
    (p. 160)
1 pound ricotta or cottage
    cheese
2 tablespoons grated
    semi-sweet chocolate

2 tablespoons shredded
    orange peel
2 tablespoons sugar
3 tablespoons milk
Confectioners' sugar

Prepare the Choux Paste and bake the puffs, making

them the size of profiteroles (about 2" in diameter).

Combine the cheese, chocolate, orange peel, sugar and milk. Blend well and taste to see if the mixture is sweet enough. Cut each baked puff in half and fill the bottom half with a scant teaspoon of the mixture. Cover with the top and sprinkle with sifted confectioners' sugar. *To Serve:* Arrange the puffs on a paper doily on a round platter. Add thin slices of unpeeled orange around the platter for garnish.

WHAT TO DO WHEN

The Day Before: Prepare antipasto, cover tightly and refrigerate. Make the spaghetti sauce. While the sauce is cooking, make the Choux Paste and bake. Prepare ricotta filling and refrigerate. Do not fill the puffs; store the filling separately. Make the salad dressing.

The Same Day: An hour and 15 minutes before dinner, boil water for the spaghetti. While the water is coming to a boil, remove the antipasto, spaghetti sauce and ricotta filling from the refrigerator. Place spaghetti sauce in a saucepan over medium heat to warm. Stir occasionally. Cook the spaghetti. While the spaghetti is cooking, fill the puffs and garnish the puffs. Drain the spaghetti, add the sauce and serve immediately.

MENU FROM INDIA

India's most famous gastronomical influence is curry, a highly spiced stew with the distinctive flavor of golden yellow curry powder. It is usually accompanied by chutney, a piquant fruit dish made from mangoes, and a variety of other small side dishes, mostly fruits. An authentic Indian curry is made with spices unavailable to us and is much hotter than what most of us would comfortably enjoy. The adaptation in the following menu is easily made in advance and can be stored in the refrigerator or freezer.

Lamb Curry*
Saffron Rice (p. 96)
Calcutta Cucumbers*
Madras Carrot Sweet*

LAMB CURRY

(Makes 6 servings)

3 tablespoons peanut or
   salad oil
2 pounds boneless shoul-
   der or leg of lamb,
   cut in cubes
1 large onion, chopped
1 clove garlic, crushed
2 teaspoons curry powder

1 teaspoon salt
½ teaspoon dry mustard
   (optional)
2 tablespoons flour
½ cup applesauce
1½ cups water
2 tablespoons flaked
   coconut

Heat the oil in a heavy casserole or large saucepan. Brown the lamb on all sides, a few pieces at a time. Remove the meat with a slotted spoon and set aside.

Add the onion and garlic to the oil and cook until soft and golden. Add the curry powder, salt, mustard and flour and mix well.

Add the lamb, applesauce and water, stirring until blended. Cover and simmer 1½ hours or until lamb is tender. Stir in the coconut just before serving.

To Serve: Surround casserole with small dishes of chutney, mashed banana, peanuts, raisins and pineapple chunks.

CALCUTTA CUCUMBERS
(Makes 6 to 8 servings)

1 cucumber, thinly sliced
1 tablespoon sugar
2 tablespoons vinegar
2 medium tomatoes,
    peeled and diced

1 medium onion, minced
3 tablespoons minced
    fresh parsley
1 container (8 oz.) plain
    yogurt

Place the slices of cucumber in a small deep bowl. Spoon the sugar and vinegar over them. Let stand while you prepare the rest of the salad.

Combine the tomatoes, onion and parsley with the yogurt in a serving bowl. Drain the cucumbers and add to the yogurt mixture. Blend gently and season with 1 teaspoon salt. Taste and add more salt if necessary.

Serve chilled with the Lamb Curry.

MADRAS CARROT SWEET
(Makes 6 to 8 servings)

2½ cups milk
1 pound carrots, peeled
    and grated

1 cup rice
4 tablespoons (about)
    sugar

3 tablespoons chopped blanched almonds

Bring the milk to a boil, add the carrots and rice and cook, stirring occasionally, until thickened, about 25 minutes. Add sugar and blend well. Serve hot in a pretty bowl with the almonds sprinkled on top.

WHAT TO DO WHEN

The Day Before: Prepare the curry, cool to room temperature and refrigerate. Grate carrots for dessert. Prepare curry garnishes in small serving bowls. Be

134

sure to coat the mashed banana with lemon juice to prevent its turning brown.

The Same Day: One hour and 15 minutes before dinner, remove the curry from the refrigerator. Prepare the Calcutta Cucumbers. Preheat the oven. Prepare and cook the Saffron Rice. Reheat curry at 350° F. Prepare and cook the Carrot Sweet.

MENU FROM RUSSIA

The two most famous words in Russian cuisine are Stroganoff and Romanoff. Classic examples of both are included in the following menu. Beef Stroganoff, in which strips of steak are cooked in a tangy sour cream sauce, is so popular that almost any combination of meat and sour cream is likely to be labeled a Stroganoff.

Eggplant Caviar*

Beef Stroganoff*

Buttered Poppy seed
  Noodles

Tossed Green Salad (p. 68)

Strawberries Romanoff (p. 171)

EGGPLANT CAVIAR
(Makes 6 to 8 servings)

1 medium eggplant	3 cloves garlic, crushed
1 small green pepper, minced	1 jar (7 oz.) ripe pitted olives, chopped
1 medium onion, minced	6 tablespoons olive oil
1 to 2 teaspoons salt	

Preheat the oven to 350° F. Place the eggplant on a jelly roll pan and bake, turning once, for 45 minutes or until soft. Peel and very finely chop the eggplant to resemble black caviar or a coarse meal.

Combine the green pepper, onion, garlic, olives, eggplant and olive oil. Blend well and add salt to taste. Add more olive oil if the mixture does not hold its shape. Chill.

To Serve: Arrange the Eggplant Caviar in the center of a platter. Surround it with melba toast, small rounds of pumpernickel and garnish with whole ripe olives.

BEEF STROGANOFF
(Makes 6 servings)

The success of this dish depends upon the quality of the steak used; filet is preferable, but top sirloin is also acceptable. Mustard is a key ingredient, so be sure not to omit it. Be very careful not to overcook the meat or to hold it more than a few minutes after cooking. Beef Stroganoff must be eaten at once.

2 pounds filet of beef or
    top sirloin, cut in
    strips 2″ long, ½″
    thick
¾ teaspoon salt
1 teaspoon black pepper
¼ cup butter

2 tablespoons flour
1 teaspoon prepared mustard
1 cup beef stock or beef bouillon
½ cup dairy sour cream
1 medium onion, sliced

Season the meat with salt and pepper and refrigerate it while preparing the sauce.

Melt 2 tablespoons of the butter in a saucepan over medium heat. Blend in the flour and mustard, being careful not to brown. Stir in the stock and blend until thickened.

136

Stir in the sour cream and cook 2 to 3 minutes; do not boil. If the sauce appears lumpy, beat it with a rotary beater until smooth or put in a blender. Add salt and pepper to taste and keep warm over simmering water in a double boiler.

Melt the remaining butter in a large skillet. Brown the onions and meat quickly, 2 minutes on each side for medium rare, doing a few pieces of meat at a time. Cover the cooked meat with a plate to keep warm. Discard the onion.

Add the meat to the sauce, warm gently for 2 minutes, and serve immediately. Serve Beef Stroganoff with buttered noodles and a tossed salad.

WHAT TO DO WHEN

The Day Before: Prepare and refrigerate the eggplant, salad greens and salad dressing.

The Same Day: One and a half hours before dinner, remove Eggplant Caviar from the refrigerator. Make Strawberries Romanoff. Prepare sour cream sauce for beef. Boil water for noodles. While water comes to a boil, toss salad and garnish Strawberries Romanoff. Cook and drain noodles, toss with butter and poppy seeds, cover and keep warm.

Finish Beef Stroganoff and serve dinner immediately.

MENU FROM POLYNESIA

As wine is characteristic of French cooking and curry of Indian, so tropical fruits are the hallmark of Polynesian cuisine. Try this menu at your next luau.

Tahitian Tomato*
Polynesian Chicken with
  Pineapple*
Deep Fried Potatoes
  (p. 85)
Island Baked Bananas*

TAHITIAN TOMATO

(Makes 6 servings)

6 medium tomatoes
½ cup cooked rice
2 tablespoons onion,
    minced

1 can (8 oz.) tiny peas,
    drained
1 teaspoon salt
½ teaspoon pepper

Cut a ¼" slice from the top of each tomato, scoop out the pulp with a teaspoon and set aside. Sprinkle a dash of salt in each tomato, invert it on a paper towel and allow the tomatoes to stand for ten minutes.

Combine the rice, onion, peas and tomato pulp. Season with salt and pepper.

Fill each tomato with the rice mixture. Serve slightly chilled but not ice cold. Add any leftover mixture to a salad.

To Serve: Place a lettuce leaf on individual salad plates. Stand the tomato in the center.

POLYNESIAN CHICKEN WITH PINEAPPLE

(Makes 6 servings)

6 tablespoons peanut or
    salad oil
½ cup flour
½ teaspoon salt
¼ teaspoon pepper
¼ teaspoon paprika
6 chicken breasts, boned
    and skinned
1 medium onion,
    chopped

1 medium green pepper,
    seeded and
    chopped
Dash of Tabasco
1 can (1 lb.) pine-
    apple chunks
1 can (8 oz.) pine-
    apple juice
1 cup chicken stock
    or bouillon

1 jar (8 oz.) maraschino cherries, drained

Preheat oven to 350° F. Heat the oil in a large skillet.

Mix the flour with the salt, pepper and paprika, and dredge the chicken with the flour mixture. Sauté the chicken on both sides until golden brown. Remove to a casserole.

Sauté the onions and green pepper in the skillet until limp, about 5 minutes. Add the Tabasco, pineapple chunks, pineapple juice and bouillon. Stir well, scraping up the browned bits that stick to the pan. Simmer 5 minutes.

Pour the sauce over the chicken in the casserole, cover and cook in the oven for 35 minutes. Add the drained maraschino cherries and return to the oven for 15 minutes. Add additional salt and pepper if necessary. *To Serve:* Garnish with grated coconut and chopped parsley.

ISLAND BAKED BANANAS
(Makes 6 servings)

6 firm bananas	⅓ cup sifted dark brown
4 tablespoons butter	sugar
or margarine	6 tablespoons rum

Preheat oven to 400° F. Slice bananas lengthwise and place in a 9″ pie plate, greased with 3 tablespoons butter. Add a layer of brown sugar. Start the layers with banana slices and end with sugar.

Spoon the rum over the bananas and dot with remaining butter. Bake for 25 minutes or until bubbly and browned. Serve warm with unsweetened whipped cream.

WHAT TO DO WHEN

The Day Before: Prepare and cook chicken. Cool to room temperature and refrigerate, covered. While chicken is cooking, prepare and refrigerate Tahitian Tomatoes. Slice potatoes, place in a bowl with water to cover and refrigerate.

The Same Day: One and a half hours before dinner, remove the chicken and tomatoes from the refrigerator. Arrange the tomatoes on a platter. Thirty minutes before dinner, re-heat chicken in a 350° F. oven. Prepare and bake the bananas.

While the chicken and bananas are in the oven, deep fry the potatoas.

MENU FROM SPAIN

Spanish cooking is better known for a few outstanding dishes than for any special flavoring or ingredient. Gazpacho, a cold raw-vegetable soup made in the blender, and Paella, a combination of chicken and seafood in saffron-flavored rice, are two international favorites that were created in Spain.

Gazpacho*
Paella*
French Bread
Orange à la Valencia*

GAZPACHO

(Makes 6 servings)

1 small onion, chopped
2 cloves garlic
5 ripe tomatoes, peeled and chopped
1 medium green pepper, chopped
1 small cucumber, sliced
1 cup chicken stock or bouillon

3 tablespoons wine vinegar
2 tablespoons olive oil
1 teaspoon salt
1 cup *each* chopped cucumber, green pepper, tomato, onion and packaged croutons

Combine in the container of the blender the onion, garlic and tomatoes; blend until smooth.

Add the green pepper, cucumber, chicken stock, vinegar, oil and salt. Cover the container and blend until smooth. Season with additional salt and pepper if necessary. Chill.

To Serve: Arrange the garnishes (last item in the ingredients) in separate dishes and let your guests help themselves.

PAELLA

(Makes 6 servings)

3 tablespoons salad oil
1 broiler-fryer chicken (2 to 3 pounds), cut up
1 small onion, chopped
1 large clove garlic, crushed
3 cups chicken stock or bouillon
1 can (1 lb.) plum tomatoes, drained

1 red or green pepper, seeded and chopped
1 cup rice
¼ teaspoon saffron
2 teaspoons salt
½ teaspoon white pepper
12 jumbo shrimp, shelled and deveined
10 fresh clams in shells
1 package (10 oz.) frozen peas

Heat the oil in a large skillet until very hot. Add the chicken, onion and garlic and sauté until the chicken is golden on both sides, or about 10 minutes over moderate heat.

Add half the stock and simmer for 15 minutes. Add the tomatoes, pepper, rice, saffron, salt, white pepper and remaining stock, stir well, and simmer 5 minutes.

Arrange the shrimp, clams and frozen peas over the rice mixture. Cover and cook 15 to 20 minutes or until all the stock has been absorbed. Season with additional salt and pepper if necessary.

ORANGE A LA VALENCIA°
(Makes 6 servings)

6 large eating oranges   granulated sugar

Peel the oranges, making certain that all the white pith has been removed. Slice them in ⅛'' rounds.

Overlap the orange slices on a small serving dish and have each guest sprinkle his own portion generously with the sugar.

WHAT TO DO WHEN

The Day Before: Prepare the Gazpacho and garnishes. Refrigerate.

The Same Day: One hour and 45 minutes before dinner, prepare and cook the Paella. While the Paella is cooking, prepare oranges and arrange on serving platter.

Warm French bread in a moderate oven (350° F.). Fill soup bowls, arrange garnishes.

MENU FROM CHINA

If France has a rival as the international queen of cuisine, that rival is China. Chinese food is not as rich as European food; no butter, cream or cheese is ever used. But it is infinitely varied, subtle and flavorful.

A typical Chinese dish combines meat or seafood with one or more vegetables cooked very quickly in hot oil. Soy sauce, brown sugar and ginger are a typical combination of flavorings, although by no means the only one. Sauces are thickened with cornstarch instead of flour. Vegetables should be crisp, almost raw, and are chosen for their texture as well as for their flavor. An ideal combination would be crisp snow peas, chewy Chinese mushrooms and crunchy water chestnuts.

Soy Spareribs*
Bamboo Shrimp*
Fried Rice*
Mandarin Pineapple*

SOY SPARERIBS

(Makes 6 servings)

5 pounds spareribs
1 tablespoon dark brown sugar
2 cloves garlic, minced
¼ teaspoon powdered ginger

1 medium onion, minced
½ teaspoon salt
¼ teaspoon black pepper
1 bottle (5 oz.) soy sauce

Trim the fat from the spareribs. Mix the sugar, garlic, ginger, onion, salt, pepper and soy sauce in a large bowl. Place the spareribs in the mixture and marinate for 6 hours or overnight in the refrigerator.

Preheat the oven to 425° F. Remove the spareribs from the marinade. Place the spareribs on a baking sheet and bake for 20 minutes. Brush ribs with the marinade, reduce oven to 375° F. and bake for 20 minutes longer.

Let spareribs cool to room temperature, cut into serving pieces, and place in the refrigerator.

A half hour before dinner, preheat the oven to 350° F. Heat the spareribs in the oven for 20 minutes until they're crisp and hot.

Serve with hot spicy mustard.

BAMBOO SHRIMP

(Makes 6 servings)

4 tablespoons salad oil
2 pounds medium shrimp, shelled and deveined
1 medium onion, thinly sliced
1 can (5 oz.) bamboo shoots, drained
1 large rib celery, thinly sliced
1 medium cucumber, thinly sliced
½ pound mushrooms, thinly sliced
½ teaspoon salt
¼ teaspoon white pepper
1 cup chicken bouillon or water
2 tablespoons cornstarch
2 tablespoons water
2 tablespoons cooking sherry
3 tablespoons blanched slivered almonds
1½ tablespoons soy sauce

Heat the oil in a large skillet. Add the shrimp, onion, bamboo shoots, celery, cucumber and mushrooms. Cook, stirring constantly, for 5 minutes until the vegetables are limp and the shrimp are pink.

Add the salt, pepper and bouillon; cover and cook for 2 minutes.

Mix the cornstarch with the water, add to the ingredients in the skillet along with the sherry, and stir for 2 minutes.

Stir in the almonds and soy sauce, heat for 1 minute. Season to taste with additional salt and pepper if necessary.

FRIED RICE
(Makes 6 to 8 servings)

⅓ cup peanut oil
½ cup minced cooked ham
½ cup minced cooked chicken
½ cup minced cooked pork
½ cup green onions, thinly sliced
3 cups cooked rice
1 2-egg omelette (p. 29)
2 tablespoons soy sauce

Heat the peanut oil in a large skillet. Add the ham, chicken, pork and green onions. Sauté the mixture for 5 minutes, stirring frequently. Blend in the rice. Slice the omelette into strips 1″ long, ¼″ wide and stir into the rice mixture. Add the soy sauce.

Heat the rice until very hot. Season with additional salt if necessary.

MANDARIN PINEAPPLE
(Makes 6 servings)

1 large fresh pineapple
2 tablespoons lemon juice
3 cans (11 oz. each) mandarin oranges, drained
½ cup superfine sugar
¼ cup orange liqueur *or* 1 teaspoon orange extract
1 tablespoon slivered almonds

Cut the pineapple in half lengthwise. Cut through the green stem leaving it intact. Remove the pineapple meat and dice. Brush the insides of the shell with lemon juice.

Combine the diced pineapple, oranges, sugar and

liqueur in a bowl and marinate for 1 hour in the refrigerator. Heap the fruit into the pineapple shells.

To Serve: Arrange the pineapple on a doily on a large platter and sprinkle with slivered almonds.

WHAT TO DO WHEN

The Day Before: Cook and refrigerate spareribs. Clean and devein shrimp. Cook rice; dice ham, chicken and pork. Cook the omelette, cover and refrigerate.

The Same Day: One and a half hours before dinner, marinate the pineapple and oranges. Assemble ingredients for the Bamboo Shrimp and Fried Rice. Preheat oven.

Half hour before dinner, cook the Bamboo Shrimp; finish rice. Reheat spareribs. Fill pineapple shells.

LET THEM EAT CAKE

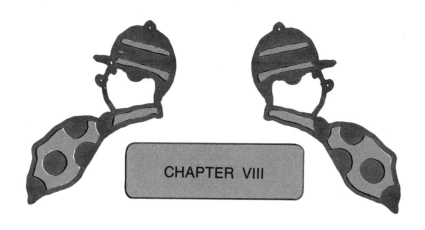

CHAPTER VIII

In deciding on a dessert, make sure you pick one that complements the rest of the meal. If the main dish is heavy or spicy, a light or fruity dessert is welcome; if the main dish is seafood or lean meat, a rich or chocolatey dessert is more appropriate. Also worth keeping in mind is whether or not you'll be free to do last-minute preparations. Scooping ice-cream balls for 24 can be tricky, for example, unless you really *like* melted ice cream or unless there's room in the freezer for 24 pre-scooped portions.

Although we have encouraged experimentation and "seasoning to taste" throughout the book, our encouragement stops with the actual baking of cakes, cookies and pastries. Here is where conformity wins over creativity. Baking is like chemistry; a single omission, addition or mis-measurement leads to unanticipated (and usually unwanted) results.

Remember, some of the most sensational desserts are crêpes and soufflés, which you can find in their own chapters.

CAKES

Cakes stand or fall on the skill of the baker. Before you begin your baking, read the following hints for better baking. They will help you avoid most of the pitfalls that plague the beginning baker.

HINTS FOR BETTER BAKING

1. Read the entire recipe before you start mixing the batter.

2. Eggs, milk and butter should be at room temperature.

3. Follow measurements exactly; see the measuring suggestions on pages 4 and 5.

4. Assemble all ingredients before you start.

5. Be sure mixing bowls are free of grease. (Egg whites won't whip well in a greasy bowl.)

6. Don't substitute salt butter if sweet butter is called for; the results can be unsatisfactory. But margarine can be substituted for butter with good results.

7. When a recipe calls for egg yolks and sugar to be beaten together until pale yellow and double in bulk, beat for 5 minutes with an electric mixer. The mixture will be fluffy and thick as a malted. *This is one of the most important steps in baking.*

8. When directed to fold in either wet or dry ingredients, be sure you fold properly (see instructions in the Glossary). Do not stir or blend or your cake will collapse.

9. To melt chocolate, which easily sticks and burns, place chocolate in a double-boiler or heat-proof dish in a saucepan of simmering water.

10. When whipping cream, be sure that the cream and the bowl are both *cold.* You can put the bowl in the refrigerator for a few minutes to chill it. Never fold whipped cream into warm ingredients or the cream will run.

BAKING DO'S AND DON'TS

Do use the correct size cake pan. If the pan is too small, the batter will overflow; if it is too large, the cake will flatten and sink in the center.

Do prepare your pan properly. Grease *lightly* (or it will smoke in the oven) with a piece of wax paper or napkin. Dust with flour, tapping out the excess. When wax paper is called for, line the bottom of the pan only, cutting the shape out with a knife right in the pan. Do all three where called for.

Don't fill your pans more than half way. Tap the filled pan gently on the work surface to remove air bubbles and distribute batter evenly.

Don't overcrowd the oven. Pans should be on the middle rack only, and should not touch.

Do test for doneness by inserting a cake tester or toothpick into the center of the cake. If it comes out clean, the cake is fully baked. This is important because baking time varies with different ovens.

HANDLING CAKE AFTER IT'S BAKED

1. Cool the cake for 5 minutes before removing from pans. Don't let it cool completely in the pans or it will

be soggy and difficult to remove.

2. Invert the pans onto a cake rack and peel off the wax paper, if it has been used.

3. Let the cake cool *completely* before frosting. A frosted cake looks more professional if the cake or the layers are upside down, with the flat surfaces facing up.

4. If you're keeping the cake more than a few hours before frosting, keep it wrapped; a damp towel will keep it from drying out. Or put it in a covered cake dish.

5. Frosted cake cuts cleanly if the knife is dipped frequently in warm water.

GENOISE French Sponge Cake
(Makes 8 to 10 servings)

The Genoise is a classic, multi-purpose cake, as light as sponge cake but much richer and more firmly textured. It can become a jelly roll, a layer cake, or a base for any fruit, ice cream or dessert sauce (or all three at once). Be sure the bowls and beater are free of grease so that the eggs and sugar will beat to more than double their volume, resulting in a light, airy cake.

6 large eggs at room temperature

1 cup *fine* granulated sugar

1 teaspoon vanilla

1 cup sifted cake flour

¼ cup sweet butter, melted

Pre-heat oven to 350° F. Lightly grease and flour two 9" or three 8" pans and line with greased wax paper. Warm the bowl and beaters from your electric mixer by soaking them in hot water for a few minutes. This will make the eggs triple in volume. Dry them well. Beat the eggs until foamy, about 2 minutes, and gradually beat in the sugar. Continue beating another 5 minutes, scrape the sides of the bowl and beat 1 minute more. Add the vanilla, and slowly fold in first the flour, then the melted butter. Pour into prepared cake pans and bake 30 minutes. Remove from pans immediately, inverting the cakes on a cake rack. Strip off wax paper. When cool, frost and fill as suggested below.

Apricot-Almond: Spread the layers and frost the sides with Chantilly Cream (p. 175). Spread apricot jam over the top layer. Press blanched slivered almonds into the sides and decorate the top with whole blanched almonds.

Chocolate-Pistachio: Spread the layers and frost the sides with Chocolate Butter Cream, (p. 176). Press chopped pistachio nuts into the sides. Frost the top with whipped cream. Pipe rosettes of whipped cream around the edge with a pastry bag. Arrange candied violets in the center of each rosette. The violets can be purchased at the gourmet food section of department stores.

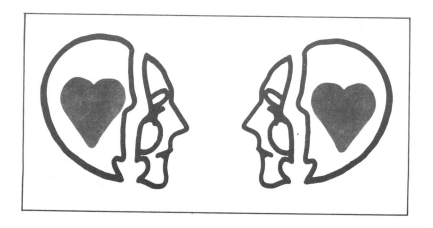

GENOISE AU CHOCOLAT   Chocolate Genoise

Add ½ cup unsweetened cocoa when adding vanilla to the basic Genoise.

Frosting: Fill layers with Coffee Butter Cream (p. 176) then gently spread a layer of whipped cream on the butter cream. Frost the cake with Chantilly Cream (p. 175) and sprinkle entire cake with finely chopped walnuts.

GENOISE A L'ORANGE   Orange Genoise

Add 2 teaspoons grated orange peel and 2 tablespoons orange juice with the vanilla.

Frosting: Fill and frost with Butter Cream flavored with orange liqueur, (p. 176). Arrange thin half slices of orange on the top of the cake and sprinkle with finely grated orange peel.

GATEAU AU CACAO   Cocoa Cake
(Makes 8 to 10 servings)

1 cup sweet butter at room temperature	6 tablespoons unsweetened cocoa
2 cups sugar	2¼ cups sifted cake flour
4 large eggs	1 teaspoon salt
	1 teaspoon baking soda

1 cup buttermilk at room temperature

Preheat the oven to 350° F. Lightly grease and flour three 8″ or two 9″ cake pans, and line the bottom with wax paper.

Cream the butter and sugar until light and fluffy by hand or electric mixer. Add the eggs, one at a time, beating well after each. Combine the cocoa, flour, salt and baking soda on a piece of wax paper. With the beater on low speed, add a little of the flour mixture, then a little of the buttermilk, alternating until all are used. Scrape sides of bowl and beat until smooth.

Pour the batter into the prepared pans and bake 35 minutes or until a toothpick inserted in the middle comes out clean.

Turn onto cake racks after 5 minutes; remove wax paper. When cool, fill and frost as desired.

Frosting: Whipped cream is delicious for both filling and frosting; use a pint of heavy cream to do both. Or fill the layers with 1 recipe of Crème Patisserie (p. 174). Frost with Coffee Butter Cream (p. 176). Sprinkle the top with shaved unsweetened chocolate.

GATEAU DE FROMAGE A L'ANANAS

Pineapple Cheese Cake
(Makes 10 to 12 servings)

2 cups graham cracker crumbs

3 tablespoons sugar

½ cup sweet butter or margarine, melted

2 cans (1 lb. each) crushed pineapple, drained

1 lb. cottage cheese at room temperature

1 lb. cream cheese at room temperature

½ cup all-purpose flour

½ teaspoon salt

1 teaspoon vanilla

1 teaspoon grated lemon peel

1½ cups sugar

6 eggs, separated

¼ cup sweet butter or margarine, melted

1 cup hot milk

Preheat oven to 325° F. Grease bottom and sides of a 9" x 3½" springform pan.

Crust: Combine graham cracker crumbs, 3 tablespoons sugar and ½ cup butter, in the cake pan. Mix and press firmly along the bottom. Bake for 15 minutes. Remove from oven and spread pineapple evenly over the crust. Let it chill while preparing the filling.

Filling: Combine the cottage cheese, cream cheese, flour, salt, vanilla, lemon peel, ½ cup of sugar, and the egg yolks in a mixing bowl. Beat at medium speed about 2 minutes, scraping sides of bowls often. Add melted butter and milk and beat 1 minute more.

In a separate bowl, beat the egg whites until foamy. Add the remaining cup of sugar and beat until the mixture forms stiff peaks. Fold the whites into the cream cheese mixture, and pour into the prepared crust.

Bake 1 to 1¼ hours on center rack, until the middle is set. Avoid opening the oven while the cake is baking. Let the cake stay in the turned-off oven, with the door slightly opened, for 1 hour after it is baked. Cool to room temperature and refrigerate. Serve chilled.

Don't be alarmed if it sinks slightly in the center; all cheese cakes do. Instead of pineapple, you may substitute 2 packages (10 oz. each) frozen raspberries or sliced strawberries, thawed and drained.

To Serve: Dust top with sifted confectioners' sugar. Arrange a pin-wheel of thinly sliced pineapple spears in center. If other fruits are used in the cake, arrange a corresponding fruit in the center.

ROULADES (ROLLED CAKES)

All the roulades are baked in a 15½ x 10½ x 1-inch jelly roll pan, lined with greased wax paper. When the cake has cooled in the pan, invert it onto a tea towel sprinkled with confectioners' sugar or powdered cocoa, according to the recipe. Peel off the wax paper, spread with the filling, and roll toward the serving platter, using the wax paper to help with the rolling.

ROULADE AUX FRAISES

Strawberry Whipped Cream Roll
(Makes 8 to 10 servings).

1 Genoise recipe (p. 152)	2 cups heavy cream
1 jar (12 oz.) strawberry preserves	¼ cup confectioners' sugar
	12 large fresh strawberries

Bake the Genoise in prepared jelly roll pan. When cool, invert onto a tea towel sprinkled liberally with confectioners' sugar. Spread with strawberry preserves and roll.

Whip the cream with confectioners' sugar, and frost the rolled cake with it. Decorate with the whole strawberries.

ROULADE A LA CONFITURE Jelly Roll

Follow the recipe for Strawberry Whipped Cream Roll, omitting the whipped cream and substituting apricot or any other jam you prefer for the filling. Sprinkle the rolled cake with confectioners' sugar and garnish with whole walnuts.

ROULADE AU CHOCOLAT   Chocolate Roll

(Makes 8 to 10 servings)

6 squares semi-sweet bak-
ing chocolate
6 large eggs, separated
¾ cup sugar
2 tablespoons liquid cof-
fee

⅛ teaspoon salt
About 4 tablespoons un-
sweetened cocoa
1 pint softened ice cream,
any flavor
1 to 2 cups heavy cream,
whipped

Preheat oven to 375° F. Grease the jelly roll pan *and* the wax paper.

Melt chocolate and set aside.

Beat the egg yolks with the sugar until they are lemon colored and thick, about 3 to 5 minutes. Blend in the melted chocolate and the coffee.

In a separate bowl, beat the egg whites with the salt until stiff but not dry. Blend about 6 tablespoons of the whites into the chocolate base, then fold in the rest of the white. Spread the mixture in the pan and bake for 15 minutes, until toothpick or cake tester inserted in the middle comes out clean.

When cool, invert the cake onto a tea towel sprinkled with the cocoa. Peel off wax paper, and spread cake with ice cream. Roll away from you; don't worry if it cracks as it rolls. Wrap in wax paper and freeze. One-half hour before serving, frost with whipped cream. Decorate with shaved chocolate or sifted cocoa.

COOKIES

PETITS GATEAUX SECS AU SUCRE

Sugar Cookies

(Makes about 5 dozen)

These can be cut in holiday shapes such as hearts

158

or Christmas trees with cookie cutters. Otherwise, cut them in 2" circles using the rim of a small glass.

½ cup sweet butter
1 cup sugar
1 egg
3 tablespoons milk

1 teaspoon vanilla
½ teaspoon salt
2 teaspoons baking powder
2 cups all-purpose flour

Beat the butter, sugar, egg, milk and vanilla in an electric mixer for 2 minutes, or by hand until well blended. Sift together the salt, baking powder and flour, add to butter mixture and blend well. Form the dough, which will be sticky, into a ball and refrigerate at least one hour.

Preheat the oven to 375° F. Roll out the dough until it is very thin, about ⅛" thick, and cut out the cookie shapes. Sprinkle with sugar and bake on an ungreased cookie sheet for about 8 minutes, or until the edges start to brown.

DELICES AU CHOCOLAT Chocolate-filled Cookies

Make sugar cookies; when cooled, make sandwich cookies with Chocolate Butter Cream (p. 176) as the filling.

ORANGINES Orange Wafers
(Makes about 2 dozen)

¼ cup sweet butter
¼ cup sugar
1 teaspoon vanilla
2 teaspoons grated
   orange peel

1 teaspoon orange juice
2 egg whites
¼ cup all-purpose flour

Preheat oven to 450° F. Beat the butter, sugar and

159

vanilla together until creamy. Stir in the orange peel and juice. Beat in the egg whites, one at a time, beating very well after each addition. Gently fold the flour into the batter.

Grease and flour a cookie sheet. Drop the batter, a teaspoon at a time, onto the cookie sheet, leaving room between each because they will spread. Bake 5 minutes or until the edges begin to brown.

To Serve: Sprinkle the warm cookies with sifted confectioners' sugar. Arrange on a platter garnished with orange slices.

PATE A CHOUX   Cream Puff Paste

These are the puffy-crisp pastry shells that will become cream puffs, éclairs and profiteroles (tiny cream puffs), depending upon size, shape and filling. They can be filled with ice cream, pastry cream or Chantilly Cream; then dusted with confectioners' sugar, topped with any frosting, or served with dessert sauce. They can also be used for hot hors d'oeuvres by filling them with mixtures of cheese, creamed seafood, mushrooms or chicken livers. Make up a batch some rainy afternoon and keep them, well wrapped, in the freezer.

1 cup water	¼ teaspoon salt
½ cup butter or margarine	1 cup all-purpose flour
4 large eggs	

Bring the water, butter and salt to a boil in a medium saucepan. Stir until the butter has melted. Remove from heat and stir in the flour all at once, beating vigorously with a wooden spoon.

Return to a moderate heat and beat until the mixture

leaves the sides of the pan and forms a stiff ball.

Remove from the heat and add the eggs, one at a time, beating until the paste has absorbed each egg before adding the next one. This is a job for strong arms, or for the electric mixer. The final paste is shiny and smooth.

Baking Cream Puff Pastry: Decide whether you want to make profiteroles (1" rounds), cream puffs (2" rounds), or éclairs (4" x 1"), or all three.

Preheat the oven to 425° F. Pipe the paste 2" apart on an ungreased cookie sheet, using a pastry bag with a plain tube; or drop it from a spoon. Leave enough room between puffs for them to spread. Bake 20 minutes, until golden brown; then reduce heat to 350° F. and bake 20 minutes more. Cool on a cake rack. This recipe makes about 15 cream puffs or éclairs or 28 profiteroles.

Filling Cream Puff Pastry: When cooled, make a small hole in the side of the puff, or cut each one in half. Using a pastry bag with a small plain tube, or a teaspoon, fill the puffs with 3 cups Chantilly Cream (p. 175), 1 pint of ice cream, or 2 cups of Pastry Cream (p. 174). Allow about 2 tablespoons of filling per puff.

PIE AND TART CRUSTS

The two basic pastry crusts are the Plain Pie Crust (Pâte Brisée) and the Sweet Tart Crust (Pâte Brisée Sucrée). They are made exactly the same way except for the addition of 1 tablespoon of sugar to the Sweet Tart Crust, which is used for French open fruit pies. The plain pie crust is used for Quiche Lorraine, and for any 2-crust pie.

The trick to making a successful pie crust can be summed up in one word: COLD. Use a cold bowl, cold hands, ice-cold water; and just to be really safe, refrigerate the dough for an hour before rolling. Otherwise, you may find the crust hard to roll without sticking and tearing.

PATE BRISEE   Plain Pie Crust

(Makes a single 9" crust. For a 2-crust pie double all ingredients except salt.)

1 cup sifted all-purpose flour

¼ teaspoon salt

¼ cup butter or margarine plus 1½ tablespoons

vegetable shortening *or* 6½ tablespoons shortening

2 to 3 tablespoons ice-cold water

Making the Dough: Combine the sifted flour and salt in a mixing bowl. Cut in the shortening and mix with cool hands until the mixture looks like course, floury granules. Avoid over-mixing. Sprinkle cold water over the dough and mix lightly with your hands until you can form a ball. Use the ball of dough to pick up any flour remaining in the bowl. If the dough is moist or sticky, flour your hands. Wrap the ball of dough in wax paper and refrigerate one hour.

Rolling the Dough: Lightly flour a pastry board or work counter, and the top of the dough. If you have used butter or margarine in the dough, it may be hard; if so, gently hit it with your rolling pin until soft enough to roll. Roll lightly, from the center outward in all directions, until the dough is ⅛" thick and 2" larger than the rim of the pie dish. If the dough sticks to the board or the rolling pin, add a little more flour where needed, brushing off excess.

Fitting it in the Pan: Have the pan ready close to the dough. Pick up one edge of the dough and roll it loosely over the rolling pin. With the dough draped around the pin, lift it to the edge of the pan and unroll it into the pan. Fit the dough snugly in the pan. Trim the excess dough from the rim of the pan by rolling the pin over the top of the pan. Use your thumbs to press the dough upward along the sides of the pan until it forms a tiny ridge above the rim of the pan. Flute the rim with fingertips or fork.

Baking the Crust: The crust may be partially baked, as for a Quiche Lorraine or an open fruit tart; fully baked, as for a pre-cooked pudding filling; or unbaked, as for a 2-crust fruit pie. To bake partly or completely, pre-heat the oven to 425° F. Prick the bottom and sides with a fork; cover the bottom of the crust with wax paper, and weight the entire surface with 4 tablespoons un-cooked rice.

For partial baking: Bake 10 minutes, remove the paper and rice and bake 5 minutes more.

For complete baking: Remove the paper and rice and bake an additional 10 minutes. The crust should just start to color for a partly baked shell, and be golden for a completely baked shell.

PATE BRISEE SUCREE   Sweet Tart Crust
Follow directions for Plain Pie Crust (above), adding 1 tablespoon of sugar with the flour and salt.

TARTE AUX POMMES French Apple Tart
(Makes 8 to 10 servings)

1 partly baked 9" Sweet Tart Crust
2 cups applesauce
½ teaspoon cinnamon
½ teaspoon nutmeg
1 teaspoon grated lemon peel
1 to 2 tablespoons (about) sugar
8 cooking apples
1 teaspoon lemon juice
⅓ cup apricot jam
1 tablespoon sugar
2 teaspoons water

Preheat oven to 375° F. Combine applesauce, cinnamon, nutmeg and lemon peel and stir in enough sugar to sweeten the mixture. Spoon into partly baked crust.

Peel, core, and halve the apples lengthwise. Holding the cut surface down against your cutting board, cut each half into slices ¼" thick. Arrange the slices, overlapping slightly, in concentric circles over the applesauce mixture, starting at the outside. Sprinkle with lemon juice. Bake on the middle rack of the oven about 30 minutes, or until apples are tender and start to brown. Remove from oven and cool 15 minutes.

To glaze: Warm the jam, sugar and water in a small saucepan and spread the mixture over the apples with a pastry brush or spoon.

TARTE AUX FRAISES Strawberry Tart
(Makes 8 servings)

1 completely baked 9" Sweet Tart Crust
2 cups Crème Patisserie (p. 174)
1 quart fresh strawberries
1 cup currant jelly
2 tablespoons water
1 tablespoon sugar

Fill the baked crust with the Crème Patisserie. Wash and hull the strawberries and arrange them on top of the cream. Warm the currant jelly with water and sugar in a small saucepan, and brush or spread over the berries. Lightly dust the top with sifted confectioners' sugar and press blanched slivered almonds between strawberries.

TARTE AUX CERISES   Cherry Tart
(Makes 8 to 10 servings)

1 partly baked 9" Sweet Tart Crust	2 eggs
	4 tablespoons sugar
2 cans (1 lb. each) pitted sweet black cherries, drained	3 tablespoons flour
	½ cup milk
	½ teaspoon vanilla

Preheat oven to 400° F. Fill the crust made in pie dish or flan pan with the cherries. Beat the eggs lightly and add sugar, flour, milk and vanilla. Beat with rotary beater until well blended. Pour over the cherries and bake 25 to 30 minutes, or until the filling has set. Serve warm, with whipped cream or vanilla ice cream if desired.

CUSTARD DESSERTS

The two basic French custards, Crème Caramel and Crème Brulée, are made with similar ingredients; but the Caramel is firmly molded and baked in the oven, and the Brulée is somewhat soft and is cooked in a saucepan.

CREME CARAMEL   Caramel Custard
(Makes 6 to 8 servings)

Caramel Base:

1 cup sugar	⅓ cup water

165

Custard:

3 cups milk

4 whole eggs plus 3 egg
  yolks

½ cup sugar

2 teaspoons vanilla

Caramel Base: Cook sugar and water in a small saucepan over moderately high heat, stirring constantly, until the mixture caramelizes or turns golden. This will take about 8 to 10 minutes. Coat the bottom and sides of a 6-cup mold, 8 individual custard cups, or a 1½-quart oven-proof dish with the caramel base. Place the dish or cups in cold water for a few minutes to set the base.

Custard: Preheat the oven to 350° F. and heat 1″ water in a shallow roasting pan in the oven while you make the custard. This is the *Bain-Marie* in which the custard will bake in its dish.

Scald the milk in a medium saucepan and set aside to cool. Beat the eggs and egg yolks together with a rotary or electric beater until blended. Beat in the sugar. With the beater on, add a little of the scalded milk; then add the remaining milk and the vanilla. Beat until foamy and pour into the prepared dish or custard cups. Place in the Bain-Marie and bake 40 minutes, or until a knife inserted in the middle comes out clean. Cool and refrigerate.

To unmold, run a knife around the sides of the custard, place a serving platter over the top, and invert onto the platter. Serve chilled but not ice-cold. Surround the crème with fresh fruit or Strawberries Romanoff (p. 171).

CREME BRULEE   Burnt-Sugar Cream
(Makes 6 servings)

Don't let the name mislead you; the brown sugar topping should not be burnt, merely melted under the broiler, which gives it a caramel flavor. When served plain, without the brown sugar, this type of soft custard is known as a *Crème Anglaise,* and is used in making English Trifle.

2 cups heavy cream	4 tablespoons sugar
4 large egg yolks	2 teaspoons vanilla
½ cup light brown sugar	

Scald the cream in a medium saucepan and set aside. Beat the egg yolks and sugar together until thick and lemon colored, about 2 to 3 minutes. Add the vanilla. Beating constantly, pour the hot cream in a slow, steady stream into the egg mixture. Beat well.

Pour into the same saucepan and cook over low heat, stirring constantly with a wooden spoon until the custard is thick enough to coat the back of a metal spoon. Cook slowly or the eggs will scramble. Pour into a serving dish, cool to room temperature, and chill in refrigerator at least 5 hours. Stop here if the custard is to be used in making English Trifle.

Preheat the broiler. Sprinkle brown sugar evenly over the custard and broil 4 inches from the heat for 4 or 5 minutes, until sugar melts and glazes. Be careful not to burn it. Chill again and serve.

TRIFLE ANGLAISE English Trifle
(Makes 8 to 10 servings)

Layers of sherry-soaked ladyfingers, jam, custard and whipped cream make an unforgettable combination. Do it all in advance, adding the whipped cream just before serving.

24 ladyfingers
1 cup raspberry or apricot
   jam
½ cup cooking sherry

1 recipe Crème Brulée
   (omitting brown sugar)
   (p. 166)
1 cup heavy cream

Line a flat-bottomed serving dish with a layer of whole ladyfingers, spread with jam, cover with another layer of ladyfingers, and sprinkle with sherry. Cover with the custard from the Crème Bruée recipe. Whip the cream. Refrigerate the Trifle and the whipped cream separately until serving time, adding the whipped cream topping at the last minute. Garnish the top with candied cherries and whole walnuts, if desired.

BAVARIAN CREAMS AND MOUSSE

A Bavarian Cream is made like Crème Bulée, with the additions of gelatin for firmness and varied flavorings. A mousse has similar ingredients, but is soft rather than firm and requires no cooking.

CREME BAVAROISE A LA VANILLE
Vanilla Bavarian Cream

(Makes 6 to 10 servings)

1 envelope unflavored
   gelatin
¼ cup cold water
3 large eggs, separated

½ cup sugar
Dash of salt
1 cup milk
3 teaspoons vanilla

1 cup heavy cream

Lightly oil a 1-quart mold. Pour the gelatin into a heat-proof cup, add the cold water and stir. Set the cup in a small skillet of simmering water and cook over moderate heat until the gelatin melts and the liquid is clear. Turn off heat but leave the cup in the water.

Beat the egg yolks until thick and lemon colored. Add sugar and salt, beating until blended. Scald the milk in a medium saucepan and add it to the egg mixture in a slow, steady stream, stirring constantly.

Return the mixture to the saucepan and cook over moderate heat, stirring, until thick enough to coat the back of a metal spoon. Remove from heat, blend in the gelatin and vanilla. Transfer to a large mixing bowl and refrigerate until the mixture begins to set, about 30 to 45 minutes.

Beat the egg whites with a dash of salt until they form stiff peaks. Fold the whites into the thickened custard. Whip the cream and fold into the mixture. Pour into the prepared mold and refrigerate at least 4 to 6 hours.

Unmold by sliding a knife all around the edge of the mold. Dip the bottom of the mold into warm (but not hot) water and count to 10. Place a chilled serving platter over the mold and invert onto the platter. If it doesn't slide out, insert the knife briefly at the edge to let a little air in. Garnish with brandied fruit and pipe rosettes of whipped cream on top.

CREME BAVAROISE AU CAFE
Coffee Bavarian Cream

Add 1 tablespoon liquid coffee or coffee liqueur with the vanilla.

CREME BAVAROISE A L'ORANGE
Orange Bavarian Cream

Add 2 tablespoons orange liqueur or 1 teaspoon orange extract instead of the vanilla.

CREME BAVAROISE AUX FRUITS

Fruited Bavarian Cream

Fold 1 package (10 oz.) frozen strawberries or raspberries, which have been thawed, drained and puréed, into the Vanilla Bavarian Cream with the whipped cream. Purée the fruit in a blender or food mill.

MOUSSE AU CHOCOLAT   Chocolate Mousse
(Makes 6 to 8 servings)

Considering how rich and delicious a mousse is, it's surprisingly easy to make. There's no cooking at all, except for melting the chocolate.

6 squares (1 oz. each) of German sweet cooking chocolate

4 large eggs, separated

1 teaspoon vanilla

2 tablespoons strong liquid coffee

½ cup heavy cream, whipped

Melt the chocolate by putting it in a heat-proof dish which has been placed in a skillet of simmering water. Set aside to cool.

Beat the egg yolks until thick and lemon colored. Beat in the vanilla, coffee and melted chocolate.

Beat the egg whites in a large bowl until they stand in peaks, and fold in the chocolate mixture. Gently fold in the whipped cream.

Transfer to a serving dish and chill at least 2 hours. Garnish with sweetened whipped cream and shaved chocolate.

Variations: Rum or orange liqueur (or 1 teaspoon rum or orange extract) may be substituted for the coffee.

FRUIT AND ICE CREAM DESSERTS

FRAISES ROMANOFF   Strawberries Romanoff
(Makes 6 to 8 servings)

1 quart (2 boxes) fresh
strawberries, washed
and hulled
½ cup confectioners' sugar

¼ cup orange liqueur
½ cup light rum
1 cup heavy cream,
whipped

Toss the strawberries with the sugar in a serving bowl. Add liqueur and rum and refrigerate at least one hour. Serve with whipped cream or vanilla ice cream. One teaspoon *each* of orange and rum extract may be substituted for the liqueur.

SORBET A L'ORANGE EN PANIER
Orange Sherbet Baskets
(Makes 6 servings)

3 oranges
1½ pints orange sherbet

Glacéed citron
Shredded coconut

Cut the oranges in half and scoop out the fruit, which can be saved for fruit salad. Fill the empty orange shells with sherbet, and garnish by pressing glacéed citron into each serving and sprinkling with shredded coconut. This can be frozen, ungarnished, until serving time.

PECHE MELBA   Peach Melba
(Makes 6 servings)

This famous dessert was created in honor of the Australian opera star, Nellie Melba. It is most luscious with fresh peaches, but you can certainly save time or beat the seasons by using canned or frozen peaches instead.

3 medium firm ripe peaches
⅓ cup light corn syrup
¾ cup orange juice
1½ pints vanilla ice cream

1 package (10 oz.) frozen raspberries, thawed and drained
3 tablespoons sugar

Plunge peaches in boiling water to cover, and boil one minute. Drain and peel the peaches, cut them in half and remove pits. Combine corn syrup and orange juice in a small saucepan, bring to a simmer and add peach halves. Cook gently, about 20 minutes, until barely tender. Drain and cool. Or use 1 can (1 lb.) freestone peach halves, drained, omitting the syrup and orange juice.

Purée the raspberries and sugar in a blender or strainer. Spoon ice cream into 6 dessert dishes, top each with a fresh or canned peach half, round side up; and cover with raspberry purée. Serve with whipped cream, if desired. This Melba sauce can be served over other fruits.

POIRE HELENE   Pear Hélène
(Makes 6 servings)

1½ pints vanilla ice cream
1 can (1 lb.) pear halves, drained

1 cup Chocolate Sauce (p. 173)

Scoop ice cream into 6 desert dishes (may be done in advance and frozen). Surround each ice cream scoop with 2 pear halves and top with Chocolate Sauce.

SAUCES, FILLINGS AND FROSTINGS AND DESSERT SAUCES

SAUCE A LA VANILLE   Vanilla Sauce
(Makes 1¼ cups)

½ cup sugar
2 teaspoons cornstarch
Dash of salt
1 cup water

2 tablespoons sweet butter, softened
2 tablespoons heavy cream
1 teaspoon vanilla

Combine the sugar, cornstarch and salt in a small saucepan. Add the water and cook over moderate heat for 5 minutes, until mixture is thickened and clear. Remove from heat and add the butter, cream and vanilla. Stir well and serve warm over cake, puddings or soufflés.

SAUCE AU CHOCOLAT   Chocolate Sauce
(Makes 2 cups)

8 oz. German sweet cooking chocolate
1 cup water

½ cup heavy cream
1 teaspoon vanilla

Simmer the chocolate and water in a small saucepan for 15 minutes, until chocolate is melted and mixture is smooth. Still cooking gently, stir in cream and vanilla and blend well.

Do not let the mixture boil. Serve hot or cold on soufflés, ice cream, cream puffs or cake.

SAUCE AUX FRUITS   Fruit Sauce
(Makes 1 cup)

1 package (10 oz.) frozen
   strawberries, peaches,
   cherries *or* raspberries
⅓ cup sugar

1 teaspoon cornstarch
Dash of salt
1 tablespoon lemon juice

Thaw, drain and purée the fruit in a blender, food mill, or force through a strainer. In a small saucepan, mix the purée with the combined sugar, cornstarch and salt. Cook, stirring over low heat, until slightly thickened and clear. Add lemon juice. Serve over ice cream, cake, puddings or Crème Caramel.

FILLINGS

CREME PATISSERIE   Pastry Cream
(Makes about 2½ cups)

¾ cup sugar
¼ cup cornstarch

2 cups milk
1½ teaspoons vanilla
4 large egg yolks

Combine the sugar and cornstarch in a heavy medium saucepan. Add the milk; cook over a moderate heat until the mixture is thick, stirring constantly with a whisk or wooden spoon. Add and blend in the vanilla.

Beat the egg yolks lightly with a rotary beater or fork. Carefully stir a small amount of the milk mixture into the eggs. Stir the egg mixture into the milk mixture, beating while you mix the two. Cook a few minutes, until the mixture is the consistency of mayonnaise.

If you are not using the Crème immediately, cut a piece of wax paper to fit right on top of it; this will prevent a skin from forming. The filling can be stored in refrigerator or freezer until ready for use.

Variations: Instead of 1½ teaspoons of vanilla, substitute ½ teaspoon vanilla plus: 1 tablespoon orange liqueur, rum, brandy, or powdered instant coffee; or 2 squares (1 oz. each) semi-sweet chocolate.

CREME CHANTILLY   Chantilly Cream
(Makes 1½ cups)

1 cup heavy cream
1 teaspoon vanilla

2 tablespoons sifted con-
fectioners' sugar

Beat the cream with an electric or rotary beater until it stands in soft peaks. Fold in the vanilla and sugar. If you like, you may add 2 teaspoons of liqueur. Use as a filling or topping for cake, as a filling for cream puffs and éclairs, or as a topping for fresh fruit.

FROSTINGS

The basic Butter Cream frosting can be used by it-self, or it can be transformed into any flavor frosting with a simple addition. The recipe will yield 2 cups, enough to frost and fill a 2-layer 9" cake. For a larger cake or more layers, increase all ingredients except the Cream of Tartar by one half; or use a whipped cream filling.

CREME AU BEURRE   Basic Butter Cream Frosting
(Makes 2 cups)

1 cup sugar
⅛ teaspoon cream of tartar
6 tablespoons water

4 egg yolks
1 cup sweet butter,
softened
1 teaspoon vanilla

Combine the sugar, cream of tartar and water in a medium saucepan. Bring to a boil over moderate heat, stirring constantly with a wooden spoon.

Reduce heat and simmer without stirring until the mixture is the consistency of very heavy syrup and spins fine threads from the raised spoon. It should read 244°F. on a candy thermometer, if you have one.

Cool the syrup. Beat the egg yolks with a rotary or electric beater until thick and lemon colored. With the beater on, gradually beat in the cooled syrup, then the softened butter and vanilla. Chill the frosting, and beat it again just before using.

Variations: Add one of the following with the vanilla:

CHOCOLATE FROSTING: Fold in gently until just mixed 2 squares melted unsweetened chocolate

LIQUEUR FROSTING: Add 1 tablespoon orange liqueur

COFFEE FROSTING: Add 6 tablespoons strong coffee instead of water

CITRUS FROSTING: Add 1 teaspoon grated lemon or orange peel plus 1 teaspoon lemon or orange juice

QUICK BUTTER CREAM FROSTING
(Makes 1 cup)

All the above variations apply to this easy frosting. The recipe will yield enough to frost, but not fill, a 9" 2-layer cake. If you want to fill the cake as well, increase all ingredients by one-half.

2 cups sifted confec-   3 tablespoons milk
    tioners' sugar   1 teaspoon vanilla
½ cup sweet butter, soft-
    ened

With your electric beater at low speed, combine all ingredients. Increase to moderate speed and beat until smooth. If the frosting looks too thin, add more sugar to thicken.

KNOW YOUR UTENSILS:
A COOK'S CATALOG OF EQUIPMENT

A complete list of kitchen gadgets would be impossible to compile and unnecessary to own. On the other hand, many respectable kitchens produce excellent results with far less than the following, so don't feel underprivileged if you can't find everything listed here in your own kitchen. What we have presented is a list of basic utensils and appliances you may need for the recipes in this book.

Blender: An electric appliance useful (but not essential) in mixing, grinding, chopping and puréeing.

Bowls: Any kind will do, but a nest of graduated sizes is most convenient. Heavy glass or aluminum is preferred.

Cake Rack: A wire rack that lets cakes, cookies and pastries cool without getting soggy.

Cake Tester: A thin metal rod for testing of cakes. If it comes out clean when inserted in the middle, the cake is done. A toothpick or a knife may be used instead.

Casserole: A fairly deep, covered, oven-proof round or oval dish used for stewing and braising, as well as casseroles. Often made of cast iron, heat-resistant glass or glass ceramic cookware that can be used over direct heat as well as in the oven.

Colander: A punctured metal bowl on a stand, used for draining liquids from foods.

Cookie or Baking Sheets: A large, flat metal sheet, handy for re-heating foods and many other uses besides baking cookies.

Rolling Pin: Essential for rolling pie crust and some other pastries.

Rotary or Egg Beater: A turning handle rotates the blades; for beating or whipping any light mixture, especially heavy cream or egg whites.

Scissors or Shears: Any household kind will do. For snipping fresh herbs and dozens of kitchen uses.

Scraper or Rubber Spatula: Used for stirring, folding and scraping, especially in a blender container and mixer bowl.

Sieve or Strainer: Fine or coarse woven wire basket with a long handle; for straining, puréeing, and removing lumps.

Soufflé Dish: A deep, round oven-proof dish, with straight sides; 1½ quart size is most convenient.

Spatulas: Narrow blade, sometimes flexible, for a variety of purposes such as frosting cakes and leveling measurements.

Spoons: Among the most useful kinds are wooden spoons for stirring and mixing, slotted spoons for removing foods from liquid, and a ladle for skimming and transferring.

Thermometers: A meat thermometer takes the guesswork out of roasting meat; insert it just to the center of the thickest part of the meat, not touching the bone. A candy thermometer is used in caramelizing sugar and other syrups and sauces. A deep fat thermometer is used for measuring the temperature of oil in deep fat frying.

Molds: Decorative metal, plastic, pottery or ceramic shapes used for molded foods. Great fun to work with, but a metal bowl can be used instead.

Pancake Turner: Long-handled tool with a broad flat base for turning pancakes, crêpes, and so forth.

Pastry Bags and Tubes: Cloth or plastic bags to which metal or plastic tips are fitted; both come in various sizes. Used for decorating cakes, filling cream puffs, Dutchess Potatoes and so forth.

Pastry or Basting Brush: For basting meat, glazing pastry and so forth.

Pots and Pans:

A. *Saucepans:* Deep, long-handled pots with covers, in three basic sizes; small (about 1½ to 2 quarts), medium (about 3 to 4 quarts), large (5 or more quarts).

B. *Soup Kettle or Stock Pot:* Large (6 to 10 quarts), double-handled, covered pot.

C. *Roasting Pan:* Oval or rectangular pan, with or without a rack. Most useful size is about 10″ × 12″ or 12″ × 15″.

D. *Skillets or Frying Pans:* Shallow, long-handled pan with cover. Useful sizes to have are 7″ and 10″.

E. *Cake Pans:* Three basic types.

   Layer-cake pans—two round or square, straight-sided pans, 8″ or 9″ size.

   Tube Pan—deep, ring-shaped pan for angel and sponge cakes.

   Springform pan—for removing cheese cake, icebox cake, etc. without inverting. 8″, 9″ or 10″ size.

F. *Pie Pans:* Round, 8″ or 9″ pans with shallow, flaring sides. Metal or heat-resistant glass.

G. *Tart or Flan Pan:* 8″, 9″ or 10″ pan with removable bottom and flaring sides, plain or fluted, for tarts and quiche.

Potato Parer or Peeler: A quick way to pare fruits and vegetables. It's also used to shave chocolate.

Cutting Board: Thick wooden board for cutting and chopping; saves counter tops from knicks and scratches.

Double Boiler: A saucepan with an insert. Water is placed in the pan itself, food in the insert so that it can warm, melt or cook over indirect heat. A 2″ or 3″ quart size is best.

Food Mill: A kind of strainer with a rotating arm to force food through for puréeing or removing lumps, solids and so forth.

Graters: Rough metal surfaces in fine, medium and coarse textures, for grating cheese, vegetables and so forth.

Jelly Roll Pan: Large metal sheet with shallow sides. Can be used instead of a cookie sheet, and many more purposes.

Knives: Many styles and sizes are available, but these three should accomodate most cooking needs:

A. *Chef's Knife* (also called a French knife)—an 8″ blade is useful for cutting, chopping, dicing and mincing.

B. *Paring Knife*—small version of Chef's Knife, for paring fruits and vegetables.

C. *Serrated Knife*—excellent for slicing fruits and vegetables; can double as a bread knife.

Measuring Cups: Glass for liquid measure; nest of graduated metal or plastic cups for dry measure. See pages 4 and 5 for more measuring information.

Mixer: An electric appliance used for mixing, beating and whipping; saves time and effort.

Wire whisk: A tool for lightly beating eggs or mixing other ingredients.

CONVENIENCE FOOD TABLE

Classic Sauce	Prepared Food	Preparation Guide
Béchamel (p. 45)	1 can (10¾ oz.) cream of mushroom or celery soup, undiluted.	Heat, strain, add ½ cup light cream, blend well. Yield 1¼ cups.
Velouté (p. 46)	1 can (10¾ oz.) cream of chicken soup, undiluted.	Heat, strain, add ½ cup chicken broth, blend well. Yield 1¼ cups.

179

Classic Sauce	Prepared Food	Preparation Guide
Mornay (p. 45)	1 can (10¾ oz.) cream of mushroom soup, undiluted.	Heat, strain, add cheese plus ½ cup light cream. Blend well. Yield 1¼ cups.
Aurore (p. 46)	1 can (10¾ oz.) cream of mushroom or chicken soup, undiluted.	Heat, strain, add purée plus ½ cup light cream. Blend well. Yield 1¼ cups.
Chivry (p. 47)	1 can (10¾ oz.) cream of chicken soup, undiluted.	Heat, strain, add herb and wine mixture plus ½ cup chicken broth. Blend well. Yield 1¼ cups.
Brown Stock (p. 42)	1 can (10¾ oz.) beef bouillon or 2 cups reconstituted dehydrated bouillon.	Use instead of stocks for sauces.
Brown Sauce (p. 48)	Concentrated beef gravy or beef gravy base.	Use in sauces requiring beef or veal gravy.
Madère (p. 49)	Beef gravy	Use in recipes instead of classic Espagnole
Tomato (p. 49)	Commercial tomato sauce.	Use in recipes requiring tomato sauce.
Hollandaise (p. 53)	6, 7 or 8 oz. commercial jar Hollandaise.	Warm, do not boil.
Bearnaise (p. 55)	Commercial Hollandaise.	Tarragon base plus prepared Hollandaise.
Mousseline (p. 54)	Commercial Hollandaise.	Heavy cream plus prepared sauce.

Classic Sauce	Prepared Food	Preparation Guide
Remoulade (p. 56)	Commercial Mayonnaise.	Add ingredients for Remoulade to mayonnaise, blend well.
Roquefort (p. 56)	Commercial Mayonnaise.	Add cheese to mayonnaise. Blend.
Piquante (p. 56)	Commercial Mayonnaise.	Add ingredients for Piquante to mayonnaise, blend.
Vinaigrette (p. 57)	Vinegar and Oil Dressing.	Use as directed.
Herb Vinaigrette (p. 57)	Vinegar and Oil Dressing.	Add herbs to basic dressing, blend well.
Ravigote (p. 57)	Vinegar and Oil Dressing.	Add ingredients for Ravigote to basic dressing, blend well.
Niçoise (p. 57)	Vinegar and Oil Dressing.	Add ingredients for Niçoise to basic dressing, blend well.

Convenience Food Equivalent

1 tablespoon instant onion	equals	¼ cup minced onion
1 tablespoon onion flakes	equals	¼ cup minced onion
⅛ teaspoon minced garlic	equals	1 medium garlic clove
1 teaspoon parsley flakes	equals	2 sprigs parsley
1 tablespoon celery flakes	equals	½ medium stalk celery
¼ teaspoon dried herb	equals	1 tablespoon fresh herb

COMING TO TERMS:
A COOKING DICTIONARY

Bain-Marie: A French term referring to a hot water bath in which certain foods, such as Crème Caramel, are baked. The bath is made by filling a shallow pan with an inch of water. The dish containing the food is placed in the bath and cooked in the oven.

Bake: Cook with dry heat in an oven. Called roasting when meat is cooked this way.

Baste: Brush or spoon a liquid over food while it is cooking to keep it from drying out.

Batter: A mixture of flour, liquid and other ingredients, used in cakes, crêpes, and so forth, as well as for coating foods before frying.

Blanch: Plunge briefly into boiling water to help loosen skin before peeling foods like tomatoes or peaches, or to remove strong tastes from foods like cabbage.

Blend: Stir ingredients until mixed.

Boil: Cook in rapidly bubbling liquid.

Bouillon: A broth made by simmering meat or vegetables in liquid. Can be bought canned or concentrated in the form of cubes or powder.

Bouquet Garni: Two or three herbs tied together so that they are easily removed from a dish after cooking.

Braise: Brown meat slowly on all sides in a little fat; then add liquid and simmer, covered, over low heat or in the oven until meat is tender.

Broil: Cook under direct heat in a broiler, or over hot coals on a grill.

Brown: Cook meat in fat over moderately high heat until surfaces are brown, to seal in juices.

Caramelize: Melt granulated sugar over medium high heat, stirring constantly, until it becomes a golden syrup.

Chop: Cut food into small pieces with a knife or food chopper.

Coat: Cover with a thin layer of flour, breadcrumbs and so forth, by dipping the food in the mixture or shaking them together in a paper bag.

Coat a Spoon: Test a liquid for thickness by seeing if it will form a film over a metal spoon.

Combine: Blend two or more ingredients together in a bowl or pan.

Dash: One or two sprinklings of a seasoning.

Dice: Cut into ¼" cubes with a sharp knife.

Dredge: Coat with flour (See Coat).

Flambé: Flame a dish just before serving by spooning liqueur or brandy over it and igniting.

Flour: Sprinkle flour lightly on dough, pastry pans or work surface.

Fold in: Method of combining a light mixture, such as beaten egg whites or whipped cream, with a heavier mixture. The lighter mixture is first spooned on top of the heavier. Using a rubber spatula, gently cut down through the center and along the bottom, bringing some of the heavier mixture up the side of the bowl and across the top. Continue this motion carefully, rotating the bowl, until lightly blended. The mixture should look streaky rather than uniform.

Fry, Deep Fat: Submerge in very hot fat or oil and cook over moderately high heat until golden brown and crisp.

Grate: Turn solid food into fine, medium or course particles by rubbing over a grater.

Gratiné: Sprinkle a dish with grated cheese and/or breadcrumbs, dot with butter or margarine and brown under the broiler.

Herb: An aromatic plant, such as tarragon, dill or parsley, cooked with food to add flavor.

Leavening Agent: Any ingredient that causes a batter to rise, such as baking powder, baking soda, yeast, or beaten egg whites.

Marinate: Let stand in a seasoned liquid, called a marinade, for a few hours or overnight.

Melt: Heat a solid food, such as butter or chocolate, until it becomes liquid.

Meringue: A mixture of egg whites and sugar, beaten until stiff and glossy, and baked.

Mince: Chop very fine with knife or food chopper.

Pare: Remove outer covering, as of apples or potatoes, with a knife or parer.

Peel: Pull off outer covering, as of bananas or blanched tomatoes.

Pinch: The amount of dry seasoning that you can pick up between your thumb and forefinger, about ⅛ teaspoon.

Poach: Cook, completely submerged, in barely simmering liquid.

Purée: Force through a fine sieve, food mill or electric blender.

Reduce: Concentrate a liquid by boiling it down until volume decreases by a specified amount.

Roast: Cook meat in dry heat in the oven.

Rotary Beater: Also called an egg beater. Used for beating eggs, cream, etc.

Sauté: Cook and brown in a small amount of fat in a skillet. The fat should be hot, the food dry, and the pan not overcrowded if the food is to brown properly.

Scald: Heat liquid until just below the boiling point.

Sear: Brown meat quickly on all sides at a high temperature to seal in the juices.

Seasoning: Any flavoring ingredient, such as salt, pepper, garlic, and so forth.

Shred: Tear or cut into small strips.

Sift: Force dry ingredients, such as flour or confectioners' sugar, through a fine sieve to remove lumps and to refine texture.

Simmer: Cook just below the boiling point; tiny bubbles should form in the liquid.

Skim: Remove surface layer of fat, scum or foam from a liquid, using the edge of a spoon or ladle.

Snip: Cut into small pieces with scissors.

Stir: Blend briskly with spoon or wire whisk in circular motion.

Steep: Let stand in liquid.

Whip: Beat rapidly with a rotary beater, wire whisk or electric mixer to incorporate air and increase volume.

INDEX

Antipasto, 130
Apple Cream (Pomme à Crème), 60
Asparagus Ravigote (Asperges Ravigote), 75
Athenian Salad, 127

Bamboo Shrimp, 146
Bavarian Creams and Mousse, 168
Béchamel. *See under* Sauces
Beef Stroganoff, 136
Bouillabaisse, 100
Braised Beef in Red Wine (Bouef à la Mode), 98
Breadcrumbs, 5
Breast of Chicken Parmesan (Suprème de Volaille Parmesan), 69
Broccoli with Anchovy Butter (Broccoli aux Anchois), 112
Broiled Grapefruit (Pamplemousse Grillée), 81
Broiled Tarragon Chicken (Poulet Grillé à l'Estragon), 108
Broiled Tomatoes (Tomates Grillées), 120
Burnt-Sugar Cream (Crème Brulée), 166
Butter, 4
Butter Cream Frosting. *See under* FROSTINGS
Buttered Noodles (Nouilles au Beurre), 123

Cakes, 150
   Apricot-Almond Genoise, 153
   Baking Do's and Don'ts, 151
   Chocolate Genoise (Genoise au Chocolat), 154
   Chocolate-Pistachio Genoise, 153
   Chocolate Roll (Roulade au Chocolat), 158
   Cocoa Cake (Gâteau au Cacao), 154
   French Sponge Cake (Genoise), 152
   Handling Cake After It's Baked, 151
   Hints for Better Baking, 150
   Jelly roll (Roulade à la Confiture), 157
   Orange Genoise (Genoise à l'Orange), 154
   Pineapple Cheese Cake (Gâteau de Fromage à l'Ananas), 155
   Rolled Cakes (Roulades), 156
   Strawberry-Whipped Cream Roll (Roulade aux Fraises), 157
Calcutta Cucumbers, 134
Canapés, Artichoke, 77
   Cucumber-Sardine, 77
   Curried Tuna, 78
   Egg-anchovy, 77
   Ham, 78
   See also Open-Faced Finger Sandwiches
Caramel Custard (Crème Caramel), 165
Chantilly Cream (Crème Chantilly), 175
   See also Fillings
Cheese and Bacon Tart (Quiche Lorraine), 67
Cherry Tart (Tarte aux Cerises), 165
Chicken with Orange Sauce (Poulet à l'Orange), 94
China, Menu from, 144
Chocolate Frosting. *See under* Frostings
Chocolate, melting of, 5
Chocolate Mousse (Mousse au Chocolat), 170
Chocolate Sauce (Sauce au Chocolat). *See under* Dessert Sauces
Citrus Frosting. *See under* Frostings
Coffee Bavarian Cream (Crème Bavaroise au Café), 169
Coffee Frosting. *See under* Frostings
Cold Potato Leek Soup (Vichysoisse), 121
Company Meals, Do's and Don'ts for, 8
Cookies
   Chocolate-filled (Delices au Chocolat), 159
   Orange Wafers (Orangines), 159
   Sugar Cookies (Petits Gâteaux Secs au Sucre), 158
Crab Mousse (Mousse aux Fruits de Mer), 74
Cream Puffs Paste (Paté à Choux), 160
   baking, 161
   filling, 161

Crême Anglaise, 167
Crêpes, basic recipe, 15
  Dessert, 18
    Flaming (C. Flambées), 20
    Jubilee, 21
    Peaches and Cream (C. Pêches
      à la Crème), 19
    Raspberry (C. Framboise), 19
    Strawberry Sundae (C. Fraises
      en Crème Glacé), 19
    Suzette, 23
    with Chocolate-Orange Sauce
      (C. Chocolat et Orange), 22
  Lunch and Dinner, 16
    Asparagus and Ham (C. As-
      perges au Jambon), 17
    Chicken-mushroom (C. Poulet
      aux Champignons), 16
    Crabmeat (C. aux Fruits de
      mer), 18
Cucumbers Vinaigrette (Concom-
  bres Vinaigrette), 60
Custards, 165

Desserts, 149
Dessert Sauces
  Chocolate (S. du Chocolat), 173
  Fruit (S. aux Fruits), 174
  Vanilla (S. à la Vanille), 173
Duchess Potatoes (Pommes
  Duchesse), 109

Eggplant Caviar, 135
Eggs, Omelettes and Soufflès, 24
  Hard-Cooked, 28
  Poached (Oeufs Poches), 25
    Benedict (Benedictibe), 25
  Scrambled (Brouillés), 26
    Variations on,
      with cheese, 27
      with ham, 27
      with herbs, 27
      with mushrooms, 27
Egg Whites, 4
English Trifle (Trifle Anglaise), 167

Filet Steaks with Mushrooms, (Tour-
  nedos Chasseurs), 118
Fillings, 173
  Chantilly Cream (Crème Chan-
    tilly), 175
  Pastry Cream (Crème Patisserie),
    174
Flour, 4

Foods, Facts on, 4
French Apple Tart (Tarte aux Pom-
  mes), 164
French Fried Potatoes (Pommes
  Frites), 85
French Peas (Petits Pois), 90
French Toasted Ham and Cheese
  Sandwiches (Croque
  Monsieur), 62
Fried Rice, 147
Frostings, 175
  Basic Butter Cream (Crème au
    Beurre), 175
  Chocolate, 176
  Citrus, 176
  Coffee, 176
  Liqueur, 176
  Quick Butter Cream, 176
Fruit and Ice Cream Desserts, 171
Fruits in Liqueur (Maçédoine des
  Fruits), 86
Fruited Bavarian Cream (Crème
  Bavaroise aux Fruits), 170
Fruit Sauce (Sauce aux Fruits). See
  under DESSERT SAUCES

Garlic Bread (Pain a l'Ail), 80
Garnishes, 9
Gazpacho, 142
Gouda Surprise (Gouda Farci), 88
Grapefruit Salad Mold (Pample-
  mousse en Gelée), 123
Greece, Menu from, 126
Green Beans Vinaigrette (Haricots
  Vinaigrette), 66

Halva, 128
Hamburgers in Red Wine (Bifteck
  Haché au Vin Rouge), 84
Hamburger Stroganoff (Bifteck
  Haché), 66
Herb Bread (Pain aux Fines Herbes),
  72
Hollandaise. See Egg-based Sauces
Hot Cheese Fritters (Beignet au
  Fromage), 113

India, Menu from, 132
Island Baked Bananas, 140
Italy, Menu from, 129

Lamb Curry, 133
Liqueur Frosting. See under Frostings

Madras Carrot Sweet, 134
Mandarin Pineapple, 147
Mayonnaise. *See* Egg-based Sauces
Menu, How Not to Plan a, 7
Mornay Sauce. *See under* Sauces
Moussaka, 126
Mushroom Stuffed Tomatoes (Tomates Farcis), 59
Mustard, 5

Noodles with Almonds (Nouilles Amandine), 104

Omelettes, 28
  Basic (au Naturel), 29
  Do's and Don'ts, 28
Onion Soup (Soupe à l'Oignon), 107
Open-faced Finger Sandwiches (Canapes Variés), 76
Orange à la Valencia, 143
Orange Bavarian Cream (Crème Bavaroise' à l'Orange), 169
Orange Sherbet Baskets (Sorbet à l'Orange en Panier), 171

Paella, 142
Pastry Cream. *See under* Fillings
Peach Melba (Pêche Melba), 171
Pear Hélène, 172
Pie and Tart Crusts, 161
Pie Crust, Plain (Pâte Brisé), 162
Pineapple Icebergs (Ananas Glacé), 69
Pineapple Salad (Salade d'Ananas), 91
Polynesia, Menu from, 138
Polynesian Chicken with Pineapple, 139
Pork Braised in Wine (Daube de Porc), 115

Quiche Lorraine. *See* Cheese and Bacon Tart
Quick Butter Cream Frosting. *See under* FROSTINGS

Raspberry Parfait (Parfait aux Framboises), 78
Ratatouille, 79
Raw Vegetable Dip (Crudités), 75
Remoulade. *See under* Sauces
Ricotta Cream Puffs, 131

Roast Leg of Lamb (Gigot d'Agneau à la Boulangère), 88
Roux. *See under* Sauces
Russia, Menu from, 135

Saffron Rice (Riz au Safran), 96
Salade Niçoise, 71
Salad, Tossing of, 6
Sauces, 44
  Brown, Madeira (S. Madère), 49
  Brown Sauce, Basic (Sauce Brune), 48
  Classic (S. Espagnole), 48
  Roux, 44
  Tomato (S. Tomate), 49
  Butter Sauces, 50
    Almond Butter (Beurre Amandine), 52
    Brown Butter (Beurre Noisette), 51
    in White Wine (Beurre Bercy), 52
    Herb (Beurre Fines Herbes), 51
  Egg-based Sauces, 52
    Hollandaise, Classical, 53
      Variations on, 54
        Orange (Maltaise), 55
        Tarragon (Bernaise), 55
        with Whipped Cream (Mousseline), 54
    Hollandaise, Quick, 54
    Mayonnaise, 55
      Variations on, 56
        Garlic-mustard (Piquante), 56
        Herb (Remoulade), 56
        Roquefort, 56
  French Dressing, Basic (Sauce Vinaigrette), 57
    Variations on, 57
      Herb, 57
      Niçoise, 57
      Ravigote, 57
  Mushroom Sauce (S. aux Champignons), 49
  Oil and Vinegar, 56
  White with Milk (Béchamel), 45
    Variations on
      Cheese Béchamel (S. Mornay), 45
      Tomato Béchamel (S. Aurore), 46

187

White, with Stock (Sauce Velouté), 46
  Variations on
    Caper, 49
White Wine (S. Chivry), 47
  Variations on
    Gratiné, 47
    S. Crème, 47
    S. Suprème 47
Sauces, Fillings and Frostings, 173
Scallops in the Shell (Coquilles St. Jacques), 110
Seasoning to Taste, 10
Shrimp in White Wine (Crevettes en Vin Blanc), 118
Shrimp Jambalaya (Jambalaya aux Crevettes), 82
Soufflés, 32
  Dessert, 37
    Chocolate (au Chocolat), 39
    Vanilla (à la Vanille), 38
      Variations on, 39
  General Hints, 33
  Main Dish, 34
    Cheese (au Fromage), 34
    Spinach (d'Epinard), 36
      Variations on, 37
  Preparing Egg Whites for, 32
Soy Spareribs, 145
Spaghetti with Meat Sauce, 131
Spain, Menu from, 141
Spicy Artichokes (Artichauts Piquants), 93
Spinach and Bacon Salad (Salade d'Epinard), 70
Split Pea Soup (Potage St. Germain), 64
Stock, 41
  Brown (Fonds Brun), 42
  Emergency Brown or White, 44

Quick Brown or White, 43
White Chicken (Fonds Blanc de Volaille), 43
Strawberries Romanoff (Fraises Romanoff), 171
Strawberry Mousse (Mousse aux Fraises), 62
Strawberry Tart (Tarte aux Fraises), 164
Stuffed Mushrooms (Champignons Farcis), 97
Stuffed Veal Scallops (Paupiettes de Veau), 102
Sugar, Brown, 5
  Confectioners', 5
Sweet Tart Crust (Pâté Brisé Sucré), 163

Tahitian Tomato, 139
Tomatoes, peeling and seeding, 6
Tomato Juice Piquante, (Jus de Tomate Piquante), 61
Tomato Salad (Salade de Tomate), 109
Tossed Green Salad (Salade Verte), 68

Vanilla Bavarian Cream (Crème Bavaroise à la Vanille), 168
Vanilla Sauce. See under DESSERT SAUCES
Veal Marengo (Veau Marengo), 121
Velouté. See under Sauces
Vinaigrette. See under Sauces

Wines and Liqueurs, 5

Zucchini Vinaigrette (Courgettes Vinaigrette), 106